D0776606

HEAVEN BOUND LIVING

LIGHT FOR THE JOURNEY

By Knofel Staton

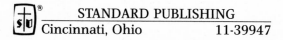

STANDARD PUBLISHING
Cincinnati, Ohio   11-39947

Sharing the thoughts of his own heart, the author may express views not entirely consistent with those of the publisher.

Library of Congress Cataloging in Publication Data:

Staton, Knofel.
  Heaven-bound living: light for the journey/by Knofel Staton.
    p. cm.
ISBN 0-87403-485-X
  1. Heaven—Christianity. 2. Christian life—1960- I. Title.
BT846.2.S7 1989   88-30533
236'.24—dc19   CIP

Copyright ©1989. The STANDARD PUBLISHING Company, Cincinnati, Ohio. A division of STANDEX INTERNATIONAL Corporation. Printed in U.S.A.

In Appreciation

In deep appreciation to Phyllis Sanders, who asked that I write on this topic and who assigned the Scriptures for ten of the chapters. And to Jonathan Underwood, who painstakingly and carefully did the editorial work at Standard Publishing Company.

The manuscript would never have reached the publishing process were it not for Julia Staton, who did the typing, and then without complaint put up with my changing completely four of the chapters and then implementing a brand new approach in many of the others.

Dedication

Affectionately Dedicated to our first grandson, Blaine Andrew, in anticipation that the joy he gives us will be multiplied by the joy he gives the Heavenly Father as he progresses on the Heaven-bound journey with Heaven-bound living, filled with the Spirit of Jesus.

THERE'S JOY IN

M - Meeting Jesus

M. Anna & Simeon MEET Jesus — Luke 2; 1-7; 21-38

T - Believing

T. A Soldier Becomes a Servant — Math. 8; 5-13

W - Thanksgiving

W. A Leper Returns To Give Thanks — Luke 17: 11-17

Th - Salvation

Th. Lydia Hears About Jesus — Matt. 28: 16-20

Acts 15: 40 — 16: 1

F. - Heaven

FR. The Journey Home — Rev. 1: 9, 10; 21: 1 —

21: 5 - 8;

Phillippians 4: 4 & 9

Without a vision (dream), the people perish.

Rainbow! Remington
Promise

Contents

1: Choose Your Destination (Matthew 7:13, 14) 11

2: Some Things Don't Change (Hebrews 13:8;
   James 1:17) 19

3: Are We Waiting for the Pilot? (John 15:5) 27

4: Your Pride Could Be Your Titanic
   (Philippians 2:5-8; Luke 2:1-38) 35

5: Winners Never Quit (Luke 2:39-52; Mark 1:9-13) . . 43

6: The Invisible and the Impossible
   (Matthew 8:5-13) 55

7: Not Bad; Just Busy (Matthew 6:5-15) 63

8: Gratitude That Gains Altitude (Luke 17:11-19) 71

9: What Are You Doing on the Way? (Luke 10:25-37) 81

10: No Pain, No Gain (Matthew 27:32; 28:7) 91

11: Grow or Die (Matthew 28:16-20) 99

12: God Will Turn Your Frowns Into Crowns
    (Revelation 21:1-8) 111

13: Watch Out for Snares and Traps (James 1:14-16) . . 117

CHAPTER ONE

CHOOSE YOUR DESTINATION

Matthew 7:13, 14

Life on earth is a journey. It is not like a carousel that we get on and go around and around and around. We are on a journey that will take us somewhere.

Once our life starts, there is no stopping. To put it in the street vernacular: "You just ain't gonna stop." You are going to keep on going forever and ever.

There is something inside human beings that knows this. As far back as we are able to study primitive cultures, we have discovered evidences that people have always been aware of an inner dream, a burning hope, a captivating desire about life that goes on—that is, a belief in the continuation of existence after physical death. Carvings on cave walls, pictures on pieces of pottery, inscriptions on animal skins—they all demonstrate a belief in a future after life on earth.

God made us that way. Although we are earth-birthed humans, we are not earth-bound humans. This is not our final destination. We are all just passing through. We are either Heaven-bound or Hell-bound. We choose which destination we will take by the journey we travel here. Since there are only two destinations, there are only two ways. Jesus spoke about them when He said, "Enter by the narrow gate; for the gate is wide, and the way is broad that leads to destruction, and many are those who enter by it. For the gate is small, and the way is narrow that leads to life, and few are those who find it" (Matthew 7:13, 14).

Not only does Jesus emphasize the two roads, but He also makes it clear that we cannot always tell whether or not we are headed in the right direction by the movement of the crowds. There are times when I am going to an event at a place I have not been before. The closer I get, the more I can follow the crowds that are heading in the same way. I have said many times, "This must be the right way because everyone else is going that way." That often applies when we are going to an event in a stadium, or to a parade, or to an air show. But that is not the criterion to use when deciding which is the way that is Heaven-bound. The fact that everyone else is going that way is no proof that they are headed in the right direction.

In fact, the opposite is true. God's people have always been in the minority. It is not difficult to discover why. The Heaven-bound road invites people to journey on it with Heaven-bound living. But do we really want to leave behind some baggage we have packed for the trip?

Which airline would you choose? The one that allows you to take all the baggage you want without any limitations or the one that restricts you to just one bag for the trip? Most of us would probably prefer the airline that has no restrictions. But are we really considering the danger we would be putting ourselves into—an overloaded plane that could lead to disaster? So it is with our journey through life.

If we desire the Heaven-bound trip, we must discard a lot of the baggage that we have been accustomed to carrying around—the baggage of poor attitudes, of bad habits, of wrong priorities, and of negative reactions. If we do not want to discard the baggage, we will never get through the "narrow gate," and we will never fit on the "narrow road."

Let's say you decide to take the airline that will let you keep all your baggage. Have you considered that airline's destination? Are you sure you want to go there for even five minutes? It is not returning; there is no way back. What if the second airline with restrictions on baggage is going precisely where you want to go and is going to the place where you want to stay forever? Now which airline will you choose? *Choose the airline, and you have chosen your destination.*

God has given each of us the freedom to choose our destination. Remember; it is a one-way journey. Whatever destination we reach, there is no return trip. Nor transfers. Nor will there be shuttles going back and forth. Wherever our journey takes us, we will be there to stay forever and ever.

The Bible speaks of those two destinies in clear terms:

Heaven-bound	*Hell-bound*
"Come, you who are blessed of My Father, inherit the kingdom prepared for you from the foundation of the world"—Matthew 25:34.	"Depart from Me, accursed ones, into the eternal fire which has been prepared for the devil and his angels"—Matthew 25:41.
"And I saw a new heaven and a new earth ... and He shall dwell among them, and they shall be His people, and God Himself shall be among them"—Revelation 21:1-3.	"And death and Hades were thrown into the lake of fire. This is the second death, the lake of fire"—Revelation 20:14.

God's given transportation vessel for our Heaven-bound journey is Jesus Christ, "I am the way, and the truth, and life; no one comes to the Father, but through Me" (John 14:6). Consequently, we do not journey alone; we are to journey toward Heaven in Christ and Christ in us. That is what He meant when He said, "Abide in Me, and I in you" (John 15:4). When we abide in Him, our journey is taking us to where His journey was taking Him. He made it clear that He was Heaven-bound. "I go to the Father," He said (John 14:28).

Jesus is the only "airline" that will take us to Heaven. It is not enough, however, just to choose the right airline. We must also decide to commit to the right living as we are in that airline. That's what Jesus was getting at when He connected His "Abide-in-Me" statement to bearing fruit (John 15:2, 5). Bearing fruit deals not with just Heaven-bound traveling, but also with Heaven-bound living.

Nothing can change the destination of the Heaven-bound airliner. But we, ourselves, must change as we are on the journey. We must change to become more like Christ. To the degree that we do not desire to change is the degree that we misunderstand the journey.

No one has the right to be born again into Christ and then keep all of his traveling baggage packed. Each of us needs to unpack what is not appropriate to Heaven-bound living and then to pack the kind of attitudes, activities, perspectives, and priorities that will be a part of living in Heaven. That's what that portion of the prayer means, "Thy will be done, on earth as it is in heaven" (Matthew 6:10). We read that our Lord is the same yesterday, today, and forever. And that's good. But we must never decide that *we* are going to be the same yesterday, today, and forever. We must change.

Our Father has made that clear to us. We are to become conformed to the image of His Son (Romans 8:29); we are to grow daily to form our character to His character (2 Corinthians 3:18); we are to become mature persons "to the measure of the stature which belongs to the fulness of Christ" (Ephesians 4:13); "we are to grow up in all aspects into Him, who is the head, even Christ" (Ephesians 4:15).

The majestic airliner of God's sovereign desire for us keeps its steady course over the ages of history. Our Lord moves undisturbed, uninterrupted, unhindered, and undistracted toward the fulfillment of the destination He desires for us in Christ Jesus. No one can hijack God's gospel ship. Nothing can cause the Captain of our destiny to alter His course, crash en route, or turn back. There will be no malfunctions on His ship, no unseen circumstances, no accidents, and no "star wars" that will bring down the ship.

But there will be storms along the way. The journey can get bumpy for us all. Our opponent, who is at the controls of the enemy ship heading toward the opposite destination, is envious and jealous that we are on board with Jesus. He will try everything he can to bring down the ship. He will not bring it down, but he will try to get us to bail out while we are on it. He will try to get us to stress our freedom so much that we become independent big shots, arrogant first-class passengers who want to have it our own way.

The enemy will try to make it uncomfortable for us in the midst of the present moral storm that has already arrived in our environment. He will try to get us hooked on some of

14

the fine sounding words, "It must be right because it feels so good"; "Everybody can't be wrong"; "Doing this just fits my created nature"; "After all, I'm just human."

The Bible uses many words to describe our Heaven-bound living on this Heaven-bound journey. Here are just a few of them:

Wait—We are to wait on the Lord (Psalm 27:14). We do not always have to be in a hurry. We are to wait for His Son to return from Heaven (Philippians 3:20). A child who does not follow his parents' orders to wait may become confused, lost, and/or kidnapped.

Walk—We are to walk "in the light" (1 John 1:6, 7); we are to walk "according to His commandments" (2 John 6); we are to walk "as He walked" (1 John 2:6).

Run—We are to run the race with Christ with certainty (1 Corinthians 9:24-26) and endurance (Hebrews 12:1).

Endure—The way can be long and tiring. But the more we are involved in the service of the Captain, it will seem shorter and smoother. We live in such an instant, touch-and-go society that endurance becomes a watchword for the Heaven-bound journey (Matthew 10:22).

Fight—But we are not to fight one another. We need to know who our enemy is (Ephesians 6:12). We are to be in the "good fight"—His fight (1 Timothy 6:12).

Flee—We are to "flee immorality" (1 Corinthians 6:18) and "youthful lusts" (2 Timothy 2:22).

Buffet—We are to get mastery over our bodies and their desires (1 Corinthians 9:27).

Draw near—Many times we want Him to draw near to us because we are not about to change perspectives, positions, or priorities—but that is inappropriate. He is the unchangeable God, and we are to draw near to Him (Hebrews 10:22; James 4:8) by making changes in what we think and do.

Imitate or mimic our Father (Ephesians 5:1).

Love—Love is other-oriented. Nothing captures Heaven-bound living more than love. If we really love, we fulfill all the intentions of the law and the prophets, for love does no harm to another person (Matthew 7:12; 22:37-40; Romans 13:8-10).

One of the most important terms that describes our Heaven-bound living is composed of just two little words:

one another. Somehow, we need to understand and live out the truth that there is only one body, one Spirit, one hope, one Lord, one faith, one baptism, and one God and Father of all (Ephesians 4:4-6).

But in the midst of that oneness, there is diversity. Each of us is different from the others. God has gifted us with individual uniqueness. Diversity among us has come out of the God over us (1 Corinthians 12:4-6). In fact, God has purposely united us by diversity so that in our differences we can minister to one another's different needs.

Because of our different backgrounds and environments and because of the different ways we think and work through problems, we are also different in our understanding of Biblical passages. As long as we are human beings with the freedom to think, there will be differences of opinions. But we must so grow in Christ that we permit our unity in Christ to be more important than our differences in various cultures (whether that be national culture, regional culture, educational culture, or denominational culture).

There is only one airline that is Heaven-bound. We must quit thinking that there is a different airline for every different doctrinal position or grouping. We are not Heaven-bound because we are in some particular group but because we are in Christ. And we can be in Christ and at the same time be in a different grouping. But we must not look at the people in another group who are in Christ as those who are not on the Heaven-bound way with us.

Paul reminded the church at Corinth that they were not independent from others but, indeed, saints along with "all who in every place call upon the name of our Lord Jesus Christ, their Lord and ours" (1 Corinthians 1:2).

None of us is Heaven-bound alone. We are Heaven-bound with Christ and *with everyone else who is in Christ.* Christ prayed that we would come to understand and live out that unity (John 17). Heaven-bound living involves living with and for one another until we all get to Heaven. After all, that's what fellowship in God's family is. Fellowship is really Christ in people benefiting people in Christ.

Those who have chosen the right airline—Jesus Christ—are headed to the right destination—Heaven. And we are headed there together. Let's act and live like it.

Is it possible that what all of us need on this journey is more grace and peace? Is it possible that is why Paul includes "grace and peace" in nearly every communication he sent to his brothers and sisters in Christ? For without grace, we could be very mean to one another and still have truth. Without peace, we could use truth (as we see it) as clubs to use in war with our brothers and sisters in the family.

Indeed, once we have begun, "there ain't no stoppin'." We are on a journey through life. As Christians, we are Heaven-bound. Some baggage will have to be left behind, but let's at least carry grace and peace with us. For in Christ, we are on the same journey with the same Captain headed for the same destination where we will stay forever and ever—with each other.

CHAPTER TWO

SOME THINGS DON'T CHANGE

Hebrews 13:8; James 1:17

A nickel double-dip ice cream cone; a twenty-five cent haircut; a movie for a nickel and thirteen milk-bottle caps; a pathway to a little two-seater house out back; a potbellied black coal stove in the center of the house for "central heat"; a clothesline with the eight-foot-by-ten-foot carpet hanging over it and a rug beater for the yearly "vacuuming"; a wringer washing machine; hand signals instead of electric turn signals on the car; hair slicked down; laundry done once a week—and not much at that; party lines (as many as eight different parties on one telephone line); one radio in the house for everyone; television—unheard of; thus was life when I was a boy.

There is one thing none of us can do. We cannot stop change. If we cannot stop changes within ourselves, then we certainly cannot stop changes outside of ourselves. And we are changing within ourselves. Just look at a picture of yourself taken twenty years ago—enough said.

But not all things change for the better. In fact, not all things change. Some of the most precious things we hold on to do not change, and we do not get tired of those unchanging things. Who really gets tired of watching the ocean waves come in and kiss the beach? The beauty of snowcapped mountains? The sunset? The sunrise that temporarily paints the sky with a special brush dipped in God's unique mixture of colors? Smelling freshly baked bread? The beauty of the outdoors under fresh-fallen snow? The

19

mellow sound of birds singing their welcoming cantata to the coming of spring? The Creator's fireworks display of the turning leaves? (The leaves are changing, but the fact that it is going to happen does not change.) Seeing cows graze gently in a meadow of emerald green? The wonder of seeing twins in a baby carriage?

Many changes touch us in our journey through life; many things do not change. One reality that does not change is Jesus Christ. He is the same "yesterday and today, yes and forever" (Hebrews 13:8). Alternate life-styles in a changing culture may tempt us to change our character. Leaders may come and go, but Jesus Christ remains constant.

That does not mean that He never changes His methods. That does not mean that He is inflexible. Indeed, He was and is innovative, creative, and flexible in His movements; but He is inflexible in His character.

There is no variableness, irregularity, fickleness, fluctuation, or vacillation in His character. His character is steady, certain, reliable, immutable, and irreversible. He is not a wave being tossed back and forth. He is not a shadow that moves with the sun. He is not a political representative who takes a survey of His constituents to see how He should vote.

The sameness of Jesus comes from His unity with the Heavenly Father. He and His Father are one. With the Father, "there is no variation, or shifting shadow" (James 1:17).

Consequently, we can trust our God on this journey through life. To say that He is the same yesterday, today, and forever is to say that He never contradicts himself. A person who contradicts himself would have to go from better to worse, or from worse to better, or from immaturity to maturity, or from maturity to immaturity.

But God cannot change for the better. He is altogether perfect. He cannot change for the worse. He is altogether holy. He cannot change toward maturity. He is altogether complete. He cannot change toward immaturity. He is "all together"—period. All that God has always been and all that God will always be is what God is now. But what is it about God that does not change?

God's Power Does Not Change

God can bring something out of nothing (the creation); He can bring nothing out of something (the end of the world); He can multiply a lot out of a little; He can heal the diseased and check the perverted. He can turn our fallen animallike instincts into resurrected Godlike characters. His power may use a song, a sermon, a good deed, a text, a mystery in nature, or a tragedy to turn us around.

God's power is available to live in us and through us as we journey through life. One of the difficulties in Christianity is that we act as if we are worshiping an impotent God. If our God is impotent, then why call on Him, why ask Him, why depend upon Him, why submit to Him? But the God of the power of Genesis 1 and the God of the power of Revelation 20 and 21 is the God who empowers our journey through life. Nothing is impossible with God.

To believe that is to become His children, who are transformed in the way we think. The moment we make up our minds that our God is the God of all power today as well as yesterday and as well as the end of the world, then we will find that we are out of adjustment to the ways the world thinks and lives.

To exalt God to the place of really being GOD is also to step out of the world's parade. It is to acquire a new viewpoint, a new and different psychology, a new and different sociology, new different science. It is to exalt Him above all-above all systems, above all philosophies, above all theories, above all priorities that grab us from time to time (people, money, possessions, or self). To exalt God is never again to give God second place to anything or any person or any idea.

God's Presence Does Not Change

God didn't create this world and then take off on a celestial coffee break to do something else while the world continued to run without Him. He is the God who is both there and here. When God declared His name as being "I am" (Exodus 3:14), He was declaring that He is always present. We don't get rid of God. There is just a small step between worshiping an impotent God and worshiping an absentee God. When God is seen as absent, our relationship to Him

21

becomes irregular, inconsistent, and inappropriate. When we worship an absentee God, our church services become very dull with no expectations. We just go through the same routines in a sort of rote memory worship. People expect to become bored and are not disappointed.

A. W. Tozer remarked that nothing can save a meeting held in the name of an absentee God. An absentee God is an inadequate God. As babies are not satisfied away from their mothers, so people are not satisfied with a long distance, remote-control, maybe-He-is-or-maybe-He-isn't available God. God did not create us to be satisfied with less than His presence. We are restless until our soul finds its identity, fellowship, and comradeship in Him.

Is it possible that the average Christian thinks of God as being at a safe distance always looking the other way? One of the assurances that God repeated time and again to His people in the Old Testament was, "I am with you" (e.g., Jeremiah 1:8). One of the promises of Jesus to Christians is, "I am with you always" (Matthew 28:20).

God's Providence Does Not Change

Regardless of the winds of the time, God is still on His throne. He allows others to go so far as a lion attached to a chain, but the chain is always measured and controlled by God himself.

No one can kick Him off the throne, and no one will. He is the Alpha and Omega. Alpha is the first letter of the Greek alphabet, and Omega is the last letter. God spoke the first letter in history, and He will speak the last letter in history. And when His final word is said, no one and no power and no counterfeit god will have anything left to say. He is not God with a small *g;* He is God with a capital *G.*

He is, indeed, "the only Sovereign, the King of kings and Lord of lords; who alone possesses immortality and dwells in unapproachable light.... To Him be honor and eternal dominion (1 Timothy 6:15, 16). He is the "Lord God, 'who is and who was and who is to come, the Almighty'" (Revelation 1:8). To fail to honor Him as the providential-sovereign God is to set ourselves up to miss being honored by Him. God made it clear that those that honor Him, He himself will honor (1 Samuel 2:20).

22

Isn't it time we quit trying to adjust God to become like us? Humanism continues to insist on trying to modify God and to bring Him nearer to man's image. Thus we enthrone man and dethrone God. Before we can say, "*Thy* kingdom come," we must say, "*My* kingdom go."

There is an old story that illustrates who is to do the changing on this Heaven-bound journey. A terrible fog had rolled in over the ocean. The captain of a ship saw a light ahead and communicated a message: "Alter your course ten degrees to the right." The message was returned to the captain, "No. You alter *your* course ten degrees to the right." The irritated captain sent back another message, "This is not just the captain of this ship. This is the Admiral of the Fleet speaking. I order you to alter your course immediately." The reply was sent, "This is not a captain of a ship speaking. This is just a seaman, but I order you immediately to alter your course." Then the third message was sent, "This is a battleship. We cannot alter quickly. Change your course at once." Then came the reply, "This is a lighthouse. We cannot change our course at all. You must alter your course now."

God is our lighthouse who cannot alter. He is the stationary providential One. As a sailor locates his position on the sea by shooting the sun, and as the pilot locates his position by the compass and cross-cultural navigational aids, so the Christian is to locate his position on this journey of life by the position of the providential God.

God's Spirit Does Not Change

The eternal Spirit is the "Holy Spirit" because He is the Spirit of the Holy God. The difference between being a Christian and a non-Christian is the indwelling presence of the Holy Spirit. Paul put it this way, "If anyone does not have the Spirit of Christ, he does not belong to Him" (Romans 8:9). The flip side of that is that if anyone does have the Spirit of Christ (earlier in the same verse called the Spirit of God), he does belong to Him.

But what is the unchanging nature of God's Spirit? Since the Spirit of God conceived Jesus, and since Jesus lived His life by the Spirit, then the Holy Spirit is like Jesus. To neglect the Holy Spirit is to neglect Christ. The contemporary neglect of the Holy Spirit in Christianity cannot be justified by the Scriptures, but only by our theological prejudices and systematic theologies. God's Spirit appears in the second verse of the first book of the Bible and in the last five verses in the last chapter of the last book of the Bible. The Holy Spirit is a part of everything between those pages.

There is a huge disparity between the place given to the Spirit in the Holy Scriptures and the place the Holy Spirit occupies in the average church today. In Scripture, the Holy Spirit is necessary, is powerful, is present, is creative, is holy, is majestic, and cannot be separated from the Father and the Son. In Jesus' humanity, He was a Spirit-anointed person. In bringing a new creation to redeem people, we are to be Spirit-anointed persons. The Holy Spirit is the third person of the Trinity—we dare not ignore one-third of the Godhead. It is possible that we in modern-day Christianity are replacing the power of the Spirit with the power of bright personalities, Madison Avenue techniques, Ph.D. credentials, and electronic razzle-dazzle.

In Scripture, the Holy Spirit is the presence of God in us and among us (Psalm 139:7). To the Holy Spirit the Scriptures attribute uniting us with God, with each other, and to our original created self, and equipping us with God's nature so we can maintain a proper relationship with both God and one another. The Scriptures reveal that the Holy Spirit teaches, supports, encourages, triggers memory, convicts, gives guidance, glorifies, intercedes for us, helps us in our weaknesses, affirms us, empowers us, gives us assurance, sanctifies us, strengthens us, implants the character of Christ in us, secures us, gives us gifts, confesses Jesus Christ, resurrects us, identifies us as God's, indwells us, gives us access to the Father, makes us fair and gentle, anoints us to meet people's needs, gives life, enables us for proclamation, helps us dethrone the deeds and idolatry of our physical bodies, justifies us, gives us visionary faith, frees us from legalism, and transforms us into Christlikeness.

It is quite clear that as we journey through this life, we are to "walk by the Spirit" (Galatians 5:16), bear the "fruit of the Spirit" (Galatians 5:22-25), set our minds on the Spirit (Romans 8:6), be "fervent in the Spirit" (Acts 18:25), "not quench the Spirit" (1 Thessalonians 5:19), "not grieve the Holy Spirit" (Ephesians 4:30), and "be filled with the Spirit" (Ephesians 5:18).

To be Spirit-filled is to be filled with the character of the Holy God and to be controlled in our actions and reactions by that character.

When the Holy Spirit moves in, our human spirits stay. We then go through the process of allowing our human spirits to decline while the Holy Spirit increases His influence and control over us.

When the Holy Spirit moves in, there is a civil war that goes on inside of us. Paul spoke about that in Romans 7 when he said, "the good that I wish, I do not do; but I practice the very evil that I do not wish" (Romans 7:19). We all experience that, don't we? I experience it. There is a difference between the desires of the "Knofel" spirit and the Holy Spirit of God living within me. The "Knofel" spirit has been around a long time. I understand the "Knofel" spirit, and I am comfortable with his decisions (although God often is not).

There are many times when the "Knofel" spirit raises his ugly head. Whenever I am sitting at a red light and it turns green and immediately I hear the person behind me honking his horn, the "Knofel" spirit wants to raise his head—and sometimes does. There are times when the "Knofel" spirit wishes I was a multimillionaire so I could put the car into reverse and slam down the accelerator. But to be filled with the Holy Spirit is to be controlled by the Spirit's unchanging character—love, joy, peace, patience, kindness, goodness, faithfulness, gentleness, and self-control (Galatians 5:22, 23). That kind of living is Heaven-bound because it's Heaven's kind of life-style, which has invaded earth's kind of life-style through God's Holy Spirit.

Now the growing questions are like these: Am I giving my mind over to the mind of God? Am I giving my voice over to the voice of God? Am I giving my desires over to the desires of God? Am I changing into the character of the God who does not change? Are you?

To do so is to activate Heaven-bound living on the Heaven-bound journey.

CHAPTER THREE

ARE WE WAITING FOR THE PILOT?

John 15:5

The journey was right on schedule until I changed planes in Phoenix. Even then it was on schedule—for a while. I got to the gate on time, and we boarded the plane on time. It was a clear, sunny day in the "valley of the sun." All the passengers got on the plane in an orderly manner and took their seats promptly.

Then we sat and sat and sat and sat. Thirty minutes later, we were still sitting. A stewardess flipped on the mike and said, "I bet you are all wondering why we are sitting here." (Can you imagine the thought entering our minds?) "Everything is ready to go, but we are waiting for a pilot to show up."

Most of the people on the plane chuckled. Here we were in a plane ready for a journey—and no pilot. I noticed something, however. No one volunteered to walk up to the cockpit and do the piloting. So we continued to wait until the pilot showed up.

Are we ever like that in our Heaven-bound journey? Are we somewhat hesitant to take the runway and soar as we were meant to soar along this Heaven-bound journey? Do we feel too much alone, somewhat as if we are playing solitaire?

Have you ever thought, "I wish someone really understood and cared." It is a touch-and-go world. We are in the fast lane. No one seems willing to take the time to look over and really see us—I mean what is inside us: our dreams, our hopes, our fears, our disappointments, our perspectives, or our feeling that we are being shelved or neglected. Sometimes it seems that the Heaven-bound road is not only narrow, but is also lonely. As we see life whirling all around us, we feel alone and inadequate.

Feeling that way, how could we take off and fly through the storms? To change altitudes, to tune in to various navigational aids, to adjust our bearings, to take quick evasive actions because the enemy is on a collision course with us, to cruise smoothly without much interruption, to stick with the flight plan when the rough air comes—can we do it?

It's one thing to talk about a Heaven-bound journey, but it is another matter if the journey involves climbing rugged mountains alone. A journey, yes—but a trip through a blinding blizzard by ourselves—that's something else.

Maybe you have heard this story or one like it. Paul Harvey tells a similar story every year at Christmastime. It's about a farmer whose family had gone to Christmas Eve services at their church—but he had stayed behind. It was one of those raw winter nights in the plains of the upper Midwest. Many of us can remember that kind of weather. It was the kind of weather that made you glad you were inside, and you hoped nothing would cause you to have to step outside. The snow was falling, not gently but meanly. Then he heard it—an irregular thumping sound against one of the windows.

He got up to see what it was. He saw tiny shivering birds— evidently attracted to the light and the warmth inside— beating against the glass in vain. It was bitterly cold, but the farmer was delightfully warm on the inside. He was touched by the plight of the birds. So he bundled himself up and trudged through the snow while the icy wind blew against him. He opened the barn door wide, he turned on the light, and tossed some hay in the corner. But the tiny birds scattered in all directions and hid in the darkness.

He tried various tactics to bring the birds into the warmth and safety of the barn. He left a trail of bread crumbs to guide them. He got behind them and tried to drive them through the open door. But nothing worked.

He finally went back to the house, thinking if got out of the way, maybe they would find the way into the barn. But the birds evidently did not understand that someone so huge could care about them. They did not sense that what he was doing was for them. He would not harm them; he would care; he would provide; he would protect; he would feed.

The farmer stared at the doomed birds from inside when a thought hit him—if he could just become like one of them for a while, then he would not frighten them. They would know that they could follow him and be safe, for he would lead them to warmth, rest, and security.

Most of us know what it means to be on the outside looking in—to be cold, tired, and lonely, to feel rejected, confused, and afraid, to scatter in all directions as we journey through this life. We may scatter into some darkness—the darkness of busyness, the darkness of bitterness, the darkness of isolation, the darkness of negative self-talk, the darkness of the fear that somebody may know, or the darkness of a negative life-style.

We have all wished it from to time—or most of us have. I wish someone could crawl inside my skin, walk in my shoes, feel the way I feel, and see things from my perspective. I wish someone could just know the pain that I'm feeling. I wish someone would take time to glance over from the fast lane and see me. I wish someone would just be with me as I am traveling through this period of my Heaven-bound journey.

But there is a gap between us, and there doesn't seem to be a bridge in sight. The good news is this—Jesus came to be that bridge. Regardless of where you are in your Heaven-bound journey, you are not alone if you are in Christ. That's why one of the first identifications of Jesus was that His name would be called Immanuel (Isaiah 7:14; Matthew 1:23). When translated, *Immanuel* means "God with us."

Notice: it is not just God above us, it is not just God ahead of us or across from us, it is not just God behind supporting us, but God WITH us as we take the runway and soar into whatever situations and through whatever situations this trip will take us.

That Jesus bundled himself up and stepped outside—yes, He left the light (where there is no night); He left the warmth (where there is no cold); He left the beauty (where there is no ugliness or meanness); He stepped outside of Heaven and began to walk WITH us.

He did it so that we could know that we don't have to be afraid of God. He did it so that we could know that God understands; God cares; God provides; God loves; God sees me; and God likes me.

He did it to let us know that as we have volunteered to start this Heaven-bound journey, the pilot has already showed up, is at the controls, and is going with us through the journey.

Regardless of where you are in your social, financial, or relational situation—know this: the pilot is on board and is WITH you.

Perhaps you are a single adult living in a couples' world. You may be single because you have never been married. Or you may be divorced or widowed. You may feel as if you are a misfit, particularly if you are on a journey with married couples sitting all around you.

However, no one knows more about singleness than He. Jesus himself was a single adult as He journeyed through life on this planet. When He needed a bit of retreat and refuge and relaxation, He came to the home of Mary, Martha, and Lazarus—all single adults. With all the families around, He chose their friendship as His refuge. God is like that for you today in your singleness.

Remember the Samaritan woman Jesus met by Jacob's well? She had probably been divorced five times and was now afraid of another commitment, but she needed a place to live and some security. So she was living with a man outside of marriage. She seemed to be ashamed of that and would not go to the well to get water at the time of day that other women went. In fact, she did not even go to the well inside the village but went outside, perhaps to avoid contact with others. Then He came—the Immanuel—God with us. He came knowing; He came caring; He came understanding. In fact, He was already there when she got to the well; He was there to meet and greet her, to seek her out. He gave her what she needed to take the runway and soar through the air in her journey. He offered her living water. He offered her something refreshing for her stagnant living, something invigorating for her burnout, something nourishing to replace the garbage she had been pouring into her life, something satisfying for the meaninglessness. (See John 4.)

Don't miss what Jesus did for her—He let her past be her past and promised her a tomorrow. He let her know that she did not have to stay on the same airline she was on. She could change airlines, pilots, and destinies. God is like that as you and I journey through life.

Have you ever turned your back on Him? We all have from time to time. When we do, we may think the Heaven-bound journey is all over. In fact, some of us may have temporarily changed airlines and think that our rebellion is irreversible. But it's not. And just so we'd know that, Jesus told a story about a rebellious boy. That boy wanted his freedom. He wanted to sow his wild oats. So off he went. He lived the opposite of how he knew his father wanted him to live. He knew better. But the TV, the magazines, and the songs made it look like such a fun, glamorous life. It probably did seem like fun at first. But it wasn't long before he found himself out of the glamour and in the gutter. Then he wanted to go home.

Sometimes it takes guts to get out of the ruts. But he had what it took. Nevertheless, he wondered whether his father would take him back. He need not have worried. The father *ran* to meet him. It is the only time we see God in a hurry in the Bible. He hurries to restore us after we take detours on our Heaven-bound journey. "Quick," the father said. That was his way of saying there is no time to lose in accepting and celebrating. Notice that the father did not ask for details about what the boy did. He was not interested in picking at the bones of the skeletons in his closet. All that mattered was that his son who had been dead because he had changed directions on his journey was alive. (See Luke 15:11-32.)

God is like that for us today in our journeys. We may have started a Heaven-bound journey but right now are not involved in Heaven-bound living. We begin to think there is no way back. Don't let the elder brothers around you put up barriers from your returning. The Father is a waiting father, a restoring father, an understanding father, a forgiving father, and a providing father.

Remember the woman caught in the act of adultery? (See John 8:1-11.) There was no guesswork about it. She was guilty. But by the time that kangaroo court was over, Jesus was standing alone with her, letting her know that her lack of Heaven-bound living did not mean that she could not continue on her Heaven-bound journey. A disastrous detour does not necessarily eliminate a Heavenly destiny.

Too insignificant to be on the Heaven-bound road? Remember the little lad with his fish and bread? Just a kid surrounded by big people in a big crowd. With Jesus, he was no longer lost in the crowd (John 6:5-13).

Feeling too important to join the "nobodies" in Christianity? Remember Nicodemus? He was probably a type A personality executive. Perhaps he was afraid of his efficiency reports at work and somewhat reluctant for his peers to know that he might be a Jesus-follower. So he came to Jesus at night (John 3).

Remember the rich man, Joseph of Arimathea—perhaps a lonely member of the upper class? It is so easy for us to forget how lonely the rich can be at times. Just how lonely is that man who drives a Mercedes to church, and his wife follows in a Jaguar, and the son in a Corvette convertible? Do they receive acceptance in the body of Christ as brothers and sisters? Are we sensitive to them and care about them? Or do we envy them? Joseph of Arimathea was searching for a way to make a difference with his wealth; he offered the tomb for Jesus' body (Matthew 27:57-60).

We are all on a journey—but does anybody know? Does anybody care? Is anybody close by? Is anybody in the pilot's seat? Is anybody willing to go all the way on this journey with us and for us?

That's the good news of Jesus. He has come, the Immanuel, God with us. We have no reason to fear or to retreat into our nights of darkness. We have no reason to scatter or to stay on the outside. Jesus has come and opened wide the doors of Heaven. The doors are open to His love, His forgiveness, His acceptance, His warmth, His understanding, and His companionship.

We are not waiting for the pilot to show up. He has come, and He is in control. But He does more than just fly the flight plan for us and get us to the destination, while we sit back and doze or watch the scenery go by. Oh, no! Our Heavenly pilot wants to equip us with His skills. He wants us to be a part of the action, participating in the lives of the people whom we pass by along the way.

While His Lordship is not up for reelection, His love is up for reincarnation. He wants to live in our skin today as He lived inside His human skin in the first century. His grace is up for reincarnation so that, through us, He can continue hearing, seeing, listening, touching, caring, noticing, forgiving, sharing with, including, longing for, and reaching out to others to help them find the right gate and begin the narrow path in the Heaven-bound journey.

No, the message is not, "We are waiting for a pilot to show up." The message is, "This is your pilot speaking." And what a pilot!

He is all-powerful.
He is all-present.
He is all-possibility.
He is all-positive.
He is all-passion.
He is all-productive.
He is all-perceptive.
He is all-prominent.
He is all-preeminent.
He is all-prosperous.
He is all-prudent.
He is all-purposeful.
He is all-pure.

He is King of the ages, of the Heavens, of glory, of time, of kings, and of the church.

He is your King and mine.

He guides.
   He guards.
      He equips.
         He cleanses.
         He heals.
            He defends.
               He conquers.
               He blesses.
                  He empowers.
                  He rewards.

He is bread to the baker.
He is light to the electrician.
He is the cornerstone to the architect.
He is the foundation to the building.
He is life to the dying.
He is the rock to the unstable.
He is the door to the excluded.
He is the physician to the sick.
He is the counselor to the confused.
He is the pearl to the jeweler.
He is the ransom to the guilty.
He is the forgiver to the sinner.
He is the joy to the downhearted.
He is the servant to the needy.
He is the master to the servants.
He is a friend to the lonely.
He is the morning star to the navigator.
He is the living water to the thirsty.
He is the seeker of the lost.
He is the revealer to the mind.
He is the spirit for the soul.

He cannot be deceived, defeated, deflated, decreased, defrauded, depleted, deposed, depressed, dimmed, diminished, discouraged, discontented, disgraced, disillusioned, disintegrated, dismayed, dissipated, or duped.

He is not deficient, demented, demeaned, debased, deplorable, depraved, disabled, discourteous, distasteful, distorted, downtrodden, dowdy, delinquent, or delirious.

He is delightful, decisive, dazzling, dear, dedicated, decent, definite, demonstrative, dependable, desirable, devoted, diligent, discerning, disciplined, discreet, and dominant.

HE IS DYNAMITE. HE IS DIVINE. AND HE IS PILOTING THIS HEAVEN-BOUND JOURNEY.

The Pilot continues speaking, "We have been cleared for takeoff."
The journey has begun. Where are you?

CHAPTER FOUR

YOUR PRIDE COULD BE YOUR TITANIC

Philippians 2:5-8; Luke 2:1-38

It had been a long day on Capitol Hill for Senator John Stennis. He was looking forward to a bit of relaxation when he got home. After parking the car, he began to walk toward his front door. Then it happened. Two people came out of the darkness, robbed him, and shot him twice. News of the shooting of Senator Stennis, the chairman of the powerful Armed Forces Committee, shocked Washington and the nation.

For nearly seven hours, Senator Stennis was on the operating table at Walter Reed Hospital. Less than two hours later, another politician was driving home when he heard about the shooting. He turned his car around and drove directly to the hospital.

In the hospital, he noticed that the staff was swamped and could not keep up with the incoming calls about the Senator's condition. He spotted an unattended switchboard, sat down, and voluntarily went to work. He continued taking calls until daylight. Sometime during that next day, he stood up, stretched, put on his overcoat, and just before leaving, he introduced himself quietly to the other operator, "I'm Mark Hatfield. Happy to help out." Then Senator Mark Hatfield unobtrusively walked out.

The press could hardly handle that story. There seemed to be no way for a conservative Republican to give a liberal Democrat a tip of the hat, let alone spend hours doing a menial task and be "happy to help out."

Such an attitude is a mark of greatness because:
Pettiness vanishes,
Pride goes,
Prejudices are erased,
Grudges leave,
"Happy to help out."

Jesus' Birth—Happy to Help Out

The first announcement recorded after Jesus' birth included, "I bring you good news of a great joy which shall be for all the people" (Luke 2:10). It is common for the birth of a baby to bring joy to the family—but to all the people? Doesn't it sound odd: a crying baby—a great joy? One boy—for all the people?

But it was so, because that boy was clothed in humility—"Happy to help out."

What happened at Jesus' birth is summarized in the second chapter of Philippians:

> Although He existed in the form of God, [He] did not regard equality with God a thing to be grasped, but emptied Himself, taking the form of a bond servant, and being made in the likeness of men (Philippians 2:6, 7).

Jesus was not detached but attached to the burdens of mankind. We can know that He cares because we can see His identity with hurting humanity when He put on flesh at His birth. John put it this way, "And the Word became flesh, and dwelt among us" (John 1:14).

The word *dwelt* literally means "pitched a tent." We might say it this way, "He bought an RV and went camping with us." Jesus wrapped himself up in human flesh and felt the burdens we feel. He brushed shoulders with us. Name your burden, and He knows about it. And He knows about it not just because He was the Creator, but also because He became one of the created ones. And He is ready to help out.

Here are some burdens/problems/heartaches that He knew about:

1. Embarrassment. Are you ever embarrassed by your identity with some family members? James Farmer tells about a wealthy woman who hired an author to write her

36

biography. The author discovered that one of her grandfathers had died in the electric chair at Sing Sing. The woman wanted that information written in such a way that that black spot in her family's past would not be obvious. So the author put the facts together in this way: "Her grandfather occupied the chair of electricity in one of America's most noted institutions. He was very much attached to his position and literally died in the harness."

Jesus' genealogy had a few black spots on it, but Jesus did not ask His biographers to hide them. He was not ashamed to make public His human pedigree. That suggests to us that He will never be ashamed of His present or future family tree, which includes you and me. Jesus is not interested in erasing names from the book of life just because someone is not perfect.

The listing of Jesus' human lineage is found in Matthew 1:1-17. That rootage includes royalty, but it also includes the common person. His rootage is interracial. Rahab and Ruth were not Jews. All of us have some interracial blood in our past if we go back for enough. To become prejudiced against another race is to misunderstand our own heritage.

Jesus' rootage included people who engaged in immorality. Judah committed incest with his daughter-in-law and thus became the father of his own grandchildren (Matthew 1:3). Rahab evidently ran a house of ill repute. David had an affair with another man's wife and manipulated circumstances so that her husband was killed. Solomon was born to that union (Matthew 1:6).

Embarrassed by your past? Jesus came to close the door to our past and to open the door to our future with Him.

2. *Family burdens.* If you could choose your parents, what characteristics would you choose? Would you like them to be mature? Would you like for them to be married? Jesus' parents were a couple of teenagers who were not married when Jesus was conceived.

Mary was greatly troubled, afraid, and puzzled when she heard what God wanted her to do. And why not? Who in the world would believe her? But Mary was willing to be seen, knowing she would be misunderstood, shamed, laughed at, ridiculed, and shunned. After all, she would be a pregnant, unmarried teenager, claiming that she was still a virgin. But she was willing to do that for Heaven's sake. When are we willing to be misunderstood, ridiculed, and laughed at because we stand up and are heard—for Heaven's sake?

What was conceived in Mary's womb was not "a thing." She was found to be "with child." Jesus' entrance into the world through a family places value upon parenting, babies, and childhood development. Have family problems? Jesus understands and is there to help out.

3. *Economic pressures.* What part of town were you from? Were you from the one-room shanties on the wrong side of the tracks or from the area of the country club and golf course? Either extreme makes no difference. Jesus left a place where the streets were paved with gold (try to find that even in the ritziest section), but put on flesh in an animals' stable.

Jesus did not come asking for a mink-lined bassinet or new blue baby clothes. He did not demand the finest rooms in the Hilton; He can be at home wherever you are.

Do you sit on orange crates? Eat off of a rickety card table? Walk on faded linoleum? Or do you sit on leather upholstery and have maids wait on you? Walk on plush carpeting? Ride in a limousine? That makes no difference. Jesus is the news of great joy to all the people.

4. *Being overlooked.* Are you a bank president? Do you own the most elite restaurant in the city? Or are you a garbage collector?

When the President of the United States visits an area, what happens? The news media is blitzed with announcements ahead of time. His airplane is accompanied by jet fighters. There is a second identical Air Force One with the same jet escorts flying a different route as a decoy. All air traffic is kept ten miles from his plane. The highest dignitaries in the area meet him when he gets off the plane, accompanied by photographers and flash bulbs. A parade of cars and limousines surrounds his ground transportation. Intersections are blocked off, and the road ahead and behind is cleared.

Anytime a head of state decides to visit a "common place," it becomes big news. Just let the President drop in on an elementary school, a commencement service, a small unaccredited college, the opening night of a midwest high school senior play, or a small Chevrolet car dealer—and watch the news media go wild!

The news media could hardly handle it when President Jimmy Carter carried his own baggage and held some village meetings where he stayed all night with a common citizen. In fact, many people criticized those decisions as pulling down the dignity of the office.

The world's Creator is coming for a visit, and who are the first to know? Not the news media, not the heads of state, not the religious, not the company presidents, not the university presidents, nor the country club set.

The King of kings has already come, and the first to know were some itinerants on the hillside who were often overlooked (Luke 2:8-10). By the time Jesus visited, respect for shepherds had taken a different route from that when King David was a shepherd boy. They were considered to be among the lowest class of people. They were migrant workers who traveled, ate, and slept with the animals—and smelled like them. It was said that all shepherd's were liars and untrustworthy. Shepherds had such a low social state that synagogues barred them from membership.

When I was a boy growing up, I remember my folks telling me to run into the house and lock the doors whenever I saw gypsies coming through town. Later, when gypsies quit traveling, the same thing was said about carnival workers when the carnival came to town. We knew how to stigmatize people then, and we still do.

The shepherds in Jesus' day were the neglected, overlooked untouchables—socially speaking. To the custodians, the street sweepers, the garbage collectors, the fruit pickers, the truck loaders of today—to you, the nobodies, the ones who are not wanted for church membership, those who are not in glamorous or well-thought-of occupations—and for you, a Savior is born. Your sins can be forgiven, forgotten, cleansed; your lives can be changed; your burdens can be lifted—misunderstandings, heartbreak, loneliness, and problems can be erased; your questions can be answered.

For He is "a Savior, who is Christ the Lord" (Luke 2:11). And He is for you today. He is available. He is accessible. He is present—for you, right now. We don't have to go through red tape; we don't have to keep at a distance—geographically, in time, or personally; we don't have to fill out application forms; we don't have to get security clearance. He is for you—today.

5. *Aging.* Sometimes the aged feel like the abandoned. Life seems to rush right past them. The music we loved changes. Traditions we counted on become rare. People we loved are dying. The world seems to belong to the young. Sometimes we can sit alone and wonder if we are really all alone. It is sometimes hard to remember that a "gray head is a crown of glory" (Proverbs 16:31) and "the honor of old men is their gray hair" (Proverbs 20:29). And as we listen to the commentators of the younger generation, we can forget that "wisdom is with aged men, with long life is understanding" (Job 12:12).

There is no preferable age category with God. To the aged He says, "Even to your old age, I shall be the same, and even to your graying years I shall bear you! I have done it, and I shall carry you; and I shall bear you, and I shall deliver you" (Isaiah 46:4).

God communicated early in Jesus' life that the aged are to be respected and valued. As was the custom, Jesus' Jewish parents took Him to the temple thirty-three days after His circumcision for the purification of the mother (Leviticus 12) and the presentation of the child to God (Exodus 13:2). The infant was presented to the priest in recognition of God's ownership. The priest, upon receiving the child, would pronounce two blessings: one in thanksgiving for the law of redemption and another for the gift of the firstborn son.

But on that day, something as significant as the presentation to the priest happened. It was God's recognition of senior citizens. Simeon was, evidently, one of those humble, pious, and relatively unknown senior citizen that live in every city. But Simeon was special. God had revealed to him that he would see the Messiah before he died.

As far as we know, he was the first person outside of Mary, Joseph, and perhaps the priest who held Jesus in his arms. And as Simeon held Jesus in his arms, he made an untraditional statement. His remarks went far beyond the cultural acceptance we normally expect from a graying

person. (Isn't it easy for us to get set in our ways and prejudices?) Simeon declared that Jesus had come for all peo-
ples, "a light of revelation to the Gentiles, and the glory of
... Israel" (Luke 2:31, 32). This favorable reference to Gentiles would have been shocking in that day. Imagine an
aged plantation owner in the deep south prior to the Civil
War putting aside all prejudice and declaring that blacks
were created equal to whites. That's the kind of impact
Simeon's remark carried.

Another person became visible in that temple area—another senior citizen. She was very old, having been widowed for eighty-four years after a seven-year marriage. She
was a woman and a prophetess. She was alone. Her whole
life was centered around the gathering place of the people
of God. There are scores of widows in the church like that
today. They live for the next time the church doors open;
then they get there early. They miss it when they can no
longer drive or see well.

God made it clear in the infancy of Jesus that He took
seriously the aged generation. We spend a lot of money to
have youth ministers, youth activities, and youth programs.
Isn't it time we began to do more in ministering to the
senior citizens through programs and activities?

The Journey of Humbly Helping

Jesus came into the world in humility—as an infant—and
in poverty, crossing all kinds of people barriers—barriers
that were beneath the dignity of the office—at least the way
some of us think.

Paul said Jesus "emptied Himself, taking the form of a
bond servant, and being made in the likeness of men," but
that's not all. He also wrote, "Have this attitude in yourselves which was also in Christ Jesus" (Philippians 2:5, 7).
What attitude? The attitude of emptying self, the attitude of
becoming a servant, the attitude of humility.

There are some things that are very hard to do: eating a
juicy grapefruit without squirting; eating "just one" good
potato chip; sleeping well when your teenager is out at
night; going into a donut shop just after a fresh batch has
been made and only asking for directions—without order-
ing a doughnut; sunning on the beach for the first time of

the year without getting sunburned; quitting smoking on the first try; driving all night without getting sleepy; picking up the ringing phone at 3 A.M. without feeling anxious; not getting irritated when that call turns out to be wrong number; and growing into the likeness of Christ without taking the journey of humility with Jesus.

No, that last one is not just hard; it is *impossible:* "Have this attitude in you which was also in Christ Jesus."

Jesus' status of being King of kings does not prevent His having empathy for us, for He has tasted of our situation. The way He loved when He was on earth is the way He still loves. He still cares about us, and He reaches out to us.

Marion Anderson was one of the greatest black singers of history. When a reporter once asked her what her greatest moment was, she could have told of many. She had been given a special award for having done the most for her hometown of Philadelphia. She had done a special White House concert for the Queen and King of England and for President Roosevelt. Her list of significant moments was long; but without hesitation, she replied, "The day I went home and told my mother she would not have to take in washing anymore." You see, she had been in a humble state. Her newfound status did not create a gap, but rather a bridge.

The greatest moment for Jesus was when your burdens were lifted at Calvary, because in His humility, you are exalted. Exalted to become a servant—looking to another and in humility saying, "Happy to help out."

The Bible makes it clear that humility is a part of Heaven-bound living. "Humble yourselves in the presence of the Lord, and He will exalt you" (James 4:10).

CHAPTER FIVE

WINNERS NEVER QUIT

Luke 2:39-52; Mark 1:9-13

Johnny Fulton was run over by a car at the age of three. He suffered crushed hips, broken ribs, a fractured skull, and compound fractures in his legs. It did not look as if he would live. But he would not give up. In fact, he later ran the half-mile in less than two minutes.

Walt Davis was totally paralyzed by polio when he was nine years old, but he did not give up. He became the Olympic high jump champion in 1952.

Shelly Mann was paralyzed by polio when she was five years old, but she would not give up. She eventually claimed eight different swimming records for the United States and won a gold medal at the 1956 Olympics in Melbourne, Australia.

In 1938, Karoly Takács, a member of Hungary's world-champion pistol shooting team and sergeant in the army, lost his right hand when a grenade he was holding exploded. But Takács did not give up. He learned to shoot left-handed and won gold medals in the 1948 and 1952 Olympics.

Lou Gehrig was such a clumsy ball player that the boys in his neighborhood would not let him play on their team. But he was committed. He did not give up. Eventually, his name was entered into baseball's Hall of Fame.

Woodrow Wilson could not read until he was ten years old. But he was a committed person. He became the twenty-eighth President of the United States.

Finally, consider this example.

At the age of seven, he had to go to work to help support his family. At nine, his mother died. At twenty-two, he lost his job as a store clerk. At twenty-three, he went into debt and became a partner in a small store. At twenty-six, his partner died leaving him a huge debt. By the age of thirty-five, he had been defeated twice when running for a seat in Congress. At the age of thirty-seven, he won the election. At thirty-nine, he lost his reelection bid. At forty-one, his four-year-old son died. At forty-two, he was rejected for a land officer role. At forty-five, he ran for the Senate and lost. At forty-seven, he was defeated for the nomination for Vice President. At forty-nine, he ran for Senate again and lost again. At the age of fifty-one, he was elected President of the United States. During his second term of office, he was assassinated. But his name lives on among the greats in U.S. history—Abraham Lincoln.

Determination, commitment, submission, and stick-to-it-tiveness—those qualities are becoming rare today. The philosophy of our times has been captured in a bumper sticker. It says, "Let's just quit." That philosophy has turned dreams into nightmares. This attitude has shattered families and devastated churches.

"When the going gets tough, the tough get going." That used to be our slogan. But now, "when the going gets tough, the tough get."

There can be no lasting commitment without submission. *Submission* has become a dirty word for many. Biblically, it means to give up self-centered interests for the benefit of others. It involves laying down one's desires to meet the needs of others, humbling oneself, and denying self in the service of others. It involves endurance.

Jesus was filled with the attitude of submission. He was submitted both to humans and to God. Heaven-bound living for us also includes being submissive to God and to other humans—to those in authority (Romans 13:1) and one another (Ephesians 5:21).

The submissiveness of Jesus did not begin the day He entered into a public ministry. It was a part of His daily lifestyle. His submissive attitude during His three-year earthly ministry was a continuation of His nature during the preceding thirty years. And He has never changed.

Submissive to Insignificant
Social and Religious Surroundings

Mary, Joseph, and Jesus returned to Nazareth after their time of refuge in Egypt. The area of Galilee and the city of Nazareth were not looked upon with high esteem by the Jewish leaders. There was a saying among the Jews that if a person wanted to be wise he should "come south—to Judea...."

Judea was seen as the pure area, while Galilee was seen as impure. Many foreigners passed through Galilee, so it was seen as the area of the Gentiles. It was declared that the social climate of Galilee was not favorable for people who had a passion for rabbinic study. The people of Galilee were seen as more religiously liberal, for they did not stick with all the traditions of orthodox Judaism.

Galilee was an agricultural area; the cost of living was about one-fifth that of Judea. It was also a center for commercial industry and trade, with a major highway system that brought people from all parts of the world.

Nazareth was considered to be such an insignificant city that Nathanael's first observation about Jesus was, "Can any good thing come out of Nazareth?" (John 1:46).

If you want to become a great ballplayer, wouldn't it make sense to move to an area that had a good sports program? I have known of some parents who moved their families to a different school district, to a different city, and even to a different state to help guarantee the development of the talents of their children. I know one family who sent their child to live with other families and in other locations so the child could study under certain teachers to realize the child's full potential and be in the Olympics.

Neither Joseph nor Mary thought that Jesus' success would be determined by the location of His upbringing. And evidently Jesus did not bug them to change locations. What some would have seen as a disadvantage to Jesus became a significant advantage. By living in Nazareth of Galilee, He was able to brush shoulders with all kinds of people—Jews and Gentiles; orthodox and liberal Jews; merchants and farmers; employers and employees.

He could observe how vines grew, the nature of branches, and the characteristics of fruit. He could see the lilies on the

45

hillside; he could watch women putting leaven in meal. He knew what it felt like to be the brunt of others' jokes; He got a taste of the value of seeing people through the eyes of God and not through the colored glasses of society.

When Jesus got old enough to leave Nazareth, He did not immediately do so. Jesus teaches us that what we become depends more upon the inward reality than upon our surrounding geography. We can develop into the kind of people God wants us to be regardless of where we live. We can't blame our hometown or our school district or anyone else for our failures. Nor can we give them total credit for our successes. We are all partially conditioned by what surrounds us, but we are never determined by it.

Jesus made the best of His surroundings. He learned from His world, even though it was thought to be inferior and small. Many of His parables related to His experiences in that world.

Submission to an Educational System

Real greatness has come out of one-room school buildings as well as out of Harvard. Greatness does not come from denying one and affirming another.

Jesus' folks could have kept Jesus away from school and taught Him themselves for fear that others might contaminate their son, who was conceived by the Holy Spirit. But they did not do that.

They started Jesus' life by conforming in every way to the Law (Luke 2:39), and there is no indication that they ever departed from any of the Jewish customs. There is no hint He continued to grow through any different process from that of any other boy in His day. In fact, the words "the Child *continued to grow and become strong, increasing in wisdom*" (Luke 2:40; cf. Luke 2:52) seem to communicate the normal developmental process for Jesus.

Jesus' first teachers would have been His parents. He would have learned as any other child learns—from observation and from listening. He would not have been too old before He learned about His circumcision, which tied Him to God's covenant.

The parents' first wish for their children in those days was "that they might live godly, soberly, and righteously in

46

the present world." Concerned Jewish parents taught in ways that would make that wish become reality.

Jesus would have noticed how His parents observed the various Jewish rituals, prayer times, festival seasons, and certain Jewish customs, such as attaching the name of God on a piece of folded parchment, which was reverently touched by everyone who entered the house.

The first religious education for a child would come from the child's mother. The Talmud affirms this by stating that the knowledge of the Law may be looked for from those who sucked it in at their mother's breast. Jesus would have heard His mother sing hymns, read the Torah, and fulfill religious duties such as preparing the Sabbath meal, preparing the Sabbath lamp, cleaning the house of leaven at Passover time, and others.

Jesus would not have forgotten or lowered His respect for womankind and their impact on the development of all children, including boys—who would, of course, become men. Consequently, He did not look down upon women as inferior when He became an adult male. Jesus remembered the significant ability of women for teaching; that is probably why He did not hesitate to teach women as well as men. In fact, He gave to women the first responsibility of telling His disciples that He had risen from the dead.

Long before He could go to school or the synagogue, He learned about praising and worshiping God and the history of Israel through the traditions and rituals practiced in His home. Every Jewish home would connect every season of the year to religious instruction about God. For instance, in midwinter, there was festive illumination in every home. The first night, only one candle was lit; the second night, two, and so on until the eighth day. This was done to teach the children about the dedication of the temple when it was restored to Jewish use after foreign domination.

In early spring, families celebrated the time of *Purim,* the feast of Esther and the nation's deliverance through her. This was a time of tremendous celebration for what that woman did for the nation of Israel.

The Passover was celebrated in the spring, followed by the Feast of Weeks. When summer came, Jewish homes used the reality of the ripened fruit to teach their children that the first and best of all fruit should be dedicated to God.

Then came autumn and the Feast of the New Year. During this time, the children were taught that man must give an account of himself in the Book of Judgment and every person has a destiny, partly based upon his commitment and performance of either good or evil.

Then the Jewish families celebrated the Feast of the Day of Atonement and the Feast of the Tabernacles, which was a thanksgiving for the harvest that had been reaped.

While the first teaching came from the mother, it was the father's responsibility to teach his son. In fact, it was taught that every other engagement, including mealtime, should give place to the primary responsibility of teaching his son the Torah. This was considered to be the real labor into which all fathers should enter and perhaps the only labor that would prove to be fruitful.

Fathers were to cultivate their sons' memory so that the law would not depart from their sons' lives. At every birthday, sons were given special birthday texts to memorize; consequently, many of the Scriptures Jesus used in His teaching were probably ones He had memorized when He was a small boy.

At the age of five, Jewish boys attended formal schooling in the synagogue. They were taught by rabbis—doctors of the law. Between the years of five and ten, they would study the Bible exclusively, beginning with Leviticus. From ten to fifteen years of age, the boys would study the Mishnah, which was filled with oral tradition—the rabbinic interpretations of the law. At age sixteen, those boys who continued their education would enter into theological discussions concerning all that they had studied up to that point.

We know that when Jesus was twelve, He went to Jerusalem with His parents for the observance of the Passover. During that period of time, rabbis would have special lectureships in one of the court areas in the temple. The lecture would be brief, followed by questions from the listeners. The questions were not calculated to trick the rabbis or put them on the spot. Questions were asked for the purpose of learning. One of the primary methods used in rabbinic teaching was the question/answer method People would ask the rabbis questions, and the rabbis would reply. Then the rabbis would ask questions to cause the people in the audience to think through, analyze, and apply what they had heard. So it was not unusual for a boy of twelve to be in the audience asking questions of the rabbis or the rabbis asking questions of the listeners (Luke 2:46, 47).

It was at the age of twelve that a Jewish boy went through the *Bar Mitzvah,* at which time he was considered to have come of age and was declared to be a "son of the Law." One of the teachings that was demanded of a boy who had come of age was that he understand that he belonged to a community and was to be responsible to that community. Jesus would take more responsibility for the community than His teachers or His parents would ever have imagined—He would *save* the community.

It is not surprising that those who heard Jesus at the age of twelve were amazed at His understanding and at His answers (Luke 2:47). There would have been other twelve-year-olds at other times who were far above their peers and amazed others with their incisiveness. The same thing happens today. Recently, a boy graduated from Harvard University at the age of fourteen.

What may be more amazing was that Jesus evidently voluntarily submitted himself to learn from human teachers. He knew by the age of twelve that God was His Father and that the things around Him belonged to His Father, "Did you not know that I had to be in my Father's house?" (Luke 2:49).

The word *house* is not in the Greek text. A better translation would be, "Do you not know that it is necessary for Me to be in My Father's things (or in My Father's affairs)?" The emphasis in the Greek was on "it is necessary." Jesus evidently knew His calling and what His priorities needed to be at this young age. It is amazing that He would submit to human teachers at all with this knowledge.

He was listening to rabbis teach about the creation when He himself had been there and participated in it. He was listening to rabbis tell about the application of God's involvement with the prophets and why God gave certain laws when He had been there and knew all about it. Nevertheless, He carried out the customary process of a boy of

His age; He sat under the rabbis without putting those rabbis down. He did not try to trick them or test them. And yet eighteen years later, they with those dark motives, questioned Him.

What a lesson for us to learn today! Sometimes we can sit under a Bible-school teacher or a preacher and feel that we know more about the topic that he does. Some people may decide to not come to Bible school because they are more advanced than the teacher. Sometimes Bible college or seminary students will decide after the first year that they know more than their teachers back home and will sleep in during the Bible-school hour. Regardless of how much we have learned or how correct we are in our understanding, there is always more to learn from others. If we don't actually learn anything new in that class session, we will be modeling right attitudes for others to follow by being a part of the class and being responsible for it. We are not to be Lone Ranger Christians.

All of us are to remain as children (without being childish), who are humble enough to be teachable. Jesus went through that passage of life. No wonder He could later say that the greatest among people are the children (Matthew 18:3, 4). Indeed, submission is an inescapable stepping stone to greatness.

Submission to Parents

It would be easy to overlook what happened after Jesus' experience in the temple at the age of twelve when He communicated with His parents that He should be about His Father's things. He did not at that time break away from them as if He had no more responsibility to them. Instead, He went back home with them and "continued in subjection to them" (Luke 2:51). What a model of submission! What an example for us to follow!

Jesus evidently had more spiritual insight at the age of twelve than His adult parents had. But He did not belittle them or think that they were second-rate or inferior to Him. There are many growing children who know more than their parents about several areas: computers, math, and science, to name a few. In this country, there are many ethnic families in which the parents do not speak English while the children are fluently bilingual. That can create family problems as the children begin to look down upon the parents for not being culturally competent. Those children are learning things in school that the parents never heard of nor will they ever understand completely. But regardless of the knowledge gap, of the cultural gap, of the spiritual gap, children are to be in subjection to their parents.

Jesus modeled what He later taught to the Pharisees, that they were to honor their mothers and fathers (Matthew 15:4-6), and what Paul taught, "Children, obey your parents in the Lord, for this is right" (Ephesians 6:1). Obedience involves action; honoring involves the right attitude. To obey literally means to "hear under"—to listen with attentiveness, to respond to what is heard.

Honoring parents calls for children to do whatever is necessary to show respect to them. We honor our parents by remembering them on special occasions, doing unexpected nice things for them, staying in contact with them even when we are away from home, keeping them up-to-date on the developments in our lives, praying for them, making daily decisions that do not violate the moral characteristics with which we were raised, forgiving them for the ways they disappointed us, saying "I love you," being physically affectionate, having celebrations on their birthdays and anniversaries, checking up on their needs, and providing for their physical and financial needs when they are old.

Jesus' respect for His parents continued throughout His life. On the cross, He gave special attention and care to His mother, whom He knew was hurting as much emotionally as He was physically.

It was partly because of Jesus' submissiveness that He continued to grow holistically—that is, intellectually (in wisdom), physically (in stature), spiritually (in favor with God), and socially (in favor with man). All of that requires humility and submission in relationships. None of those can happen if a person is arrogantly independent of others.

A person needs to manifest the proper attitudes toward people who teach in order to grow in wisdom. He needs to manifest the proper attitudes toward health practices in order to grow in stature. He needs to maintain the proper attitudes toward God in order to grow in favor with God. He needs to maintain the proper attitudes in relationships with others in order to grow in favor with men. Arrogant independence thwarts growth in each area.

Submission to God's Ways

Nowhere do we see Jesus' attitude of submissiveness to God's ways any better than in His baptism (Mark 1:9-11). Jesus walked approximately ninety miles in order to submit himself to baptism. But Jesus had not sinned and thus did not submit to baptism as an act of repentance. Then why did He do it?

John the Baptist asked Him that very question, and Jesus replied, "It is fitting for us to fulfill all righteousness" (Matthew 3:15). Righteousness has to do with proper relationships. Jesus understood that baptism was an expression of a relationship to God and also to man.

His baptism was a servant action that came out of a servant's heart. Here are some of the things He communicated in His baptism:

1. He would not ask others to do what He himself was not willing to do (Matthew 28:19).

2. He would declare a change in His life. Baptism separates our past from our present and future. For us today, it expresses a change from a life of sin to a life of forgiveness. In Jesus' life, the change was in the area of service. Up to this time, He had been living at home, working as a carpenter, and serving His family. Now He would leave home and serve all people.

3. He would identify with others. Although He had never sinned, He would identify with sinners, for He was tempted in every point as we are. His baptism was an indication that He was not going to minister in isolation from others. He was not going to live in a mountain retreat; He was going to move and live among the people. He could identify with the pressures and problems of man, for He was born as an infant and grew up through the normal development stages to adulthood. He lived with a family and with those types of relationships. He worked with His hands for wages.

He began His ministry by identifying with the hurts and needs of mankind (baptism); He continued His ministry by identifying with those needs by serving them. He ended His ministry by dying on the cross in an identity with alienated sinners and living at the right hand of the Father now, interceding for us because He continues to identify with us and for us.

God's response to Jesus in His baptism has more significance than at first we might have imagined. When God said, "Thou art My beloved Son, in Thee I am well-pleased" (Mark 1:11), He combined two truths from the Old Testament. *Thou art my beloved Son* comes from Psalm 2, which is a royal psalm about kingship. In that response, God the Father is declaring that this one is the King He is anointing.

The words *in Thee I am well pleased* come from Isaiah 42, which begins a long section describing God's suffering servant. In that response, God is declaring that King Jesus did not come to earth to be served, but to serve. This King came to earth not to be soothed, but to suffer.

As Jesus' baptism was His coronation to a broader ministry for all mankind, so is our baptism to be. Is it possible that we have missed that dimension in our understanding of baptism? Is it possible that we have narrowed the significance of baptism down to being baptized only for the forgiveness of sin or as an entrance into the church? We should realize that baptism is also our oath-taking ceremony for entering not just into God's privileges (salvation), but also God's purposes (service).

Every person's baptism is to be his ordination into service for God—into being God's ambassador—into functioning as God's representative—into being God's minister—for better or for worse, in richer or in poorer, in health and in sickness. And we will remain servants of God until death separates us from earth.

Baptism is our commitment that when the going gets tough, we are committed to stick and not quit.

Jesus lived out His baptism by serving mankind at personal expense. Are we living out our baptism? Is the Father saying about us, "In thee I am well pleased"? Will He be able to say, "Well done, good and faithful servant"?

It is a mark of greatness to be able to identify with others who are lesser in skill, but doing so can tap the potential of others and lift them up. Jesus still desires to do that today.

A mother and her nine-year-old son attended the concert of the famous pianist, Paderewski. The boy got impatient for the concert to begin. As his mother turned her head to talk with some friends, he slipped out of his seat and onto the stage where the impressive-looking grand piano was centered.

He walked over to the piano and began to play "Chopsticks." The crowd was irritated. People began to yell, "Get that boy away from there." Backstage, the master pianist heard the commotion, saw what was happening, and went onto the stage. He walked over to the boy, stood behind him, reached both arms around him, and began to play the counter melody to harmonize and accent the boy's efforts. As the two played, Paderewski kept whispering into the boy's ear, "Keep going. Don't quit, son. Keep on playing. Don't stop."

From Jesus' birth to His death, He identified with humanity, and He lived out what it means to relate to life on earth with humble submissiveness. And He comes today in His Spirit to be our companion—our live-in guest. In doing so, He is saying to all of us in the midst of life's situations and environments, "Keep going. Don't quit, my child. Don't stop."

We are not on the Heaven-bound journey alone. He walks with us and in us.

CHAPTER SIX

THE INVISIBLE
AND THE IMPOSSIBLE

Matthew 8:5-13

They had finally done it; they had made it to Sunday school. His dad wondered how he would relate to the class. This was the first time his son had been to Sunday School.

As soon as the class was over, the lad couldn't wait to get back together with his father. "Son, how did you like the class?"

The boy replied, "It was super—just super."

"What was so good about it?" his dad continued.

"That story about those people coming out of Egypt was awesome."

"Tell me about it, son."

"Well, those people had planned a clean break, but the Egyptians found out about it and chased them right to the sea. Things looked bad at first. But General Moses was really shrewd. He had a surprise waiting for the Egyptians. He got out his walkie-talkie and told the Israeli Air Force to drop some bombs. While that diversionary action was going on, the Israeli Navy built a pontoon bridge—and all the people crossed over to the other side.

"The Egyptians started after them on the bridge, but the bridge had been wired with explosives. When the Egyptians were in the middle of it, the whole thing blew up. All of Moses' people made it, and none of the Egyptians got across."

The father looked startled. "Is that the way the teacher told the story?" he asked.

"No, not quite," the boy replied. "But if I had told it the way the teacher told it, you would never believe it!"

Isn't that the way we are sometimes? We read about the power of God two thousand years ago but are quick to say, "That was God *then,* but not today." But God is the same yesterday, today, and forever. That means His character is the same. His purpose is the same. His priorities are the same. And His *power* is the same!

God has not lost one ounce of power from the day He created the world out of nothing. What has changed is man's perceptive faith—not God's powerful function.

While people want a God who has power, God wants a people who have faith. The Scripture says, "Without faith it is impossible to please Him, for he who comes to God must believe that He is, and that He is a rewarder of those who seek Him" (Hebrews 11:6). When the text says that something is impossible, no one can make it happen. No amount of activities, no amount of benevolence, no amount of giving of funds, no amount of perfect attendance at church—none of that will please God without faith.

Faith involves believing that God is—that is, that He is real, that He exists, that He is alive, that He is who He claims He is, with all the authority He says He has.

But believing that God exists is not enough. Faith also includes believing "that He is a rewarder of those who seek Him." He expects us to seek Him with the belief that He is able. And God honors that kind of faith.

Jesus encountered that kind of faith from an unexpected source in Capernaum. The man was powerful, but he had a soft heart. He dealt with facts, but he also knew about faith. He knew how to give orders, but he also knew how to take them. He knew how to be a leader, but he also knew how to be a follower.

The man was centurion—a military commander of at least one hundred men. But this military leader was different. He was of a part of the Roman occupation troops in a foreign land. He was a different race from that of the people of the land he occupied, and his religious background was far different from the Jewish religion.

Occupational troops often looked down upon the people in whose land they were staying. They would treat them with disrespect, as if the people were inferior. In one sense, the occupied people were a "defeated" people—at least militarily and politically. They occupied people were in submission to the authorities of the other country.

But this military leader was not angry with these foreigners whose land he and his troops were occupying. Instead, he saw they had something going for them. Somewhere along the way, he began to study, to appreciate, and to support their religion. He was so pro-Judaism that he built the synagogue in Capernaum and was personally respected by the elders of the synagogue (Luke 7:3-5).

The centurion had also heard about a Jew named Jesus, who had the power of God to heal. He was not skeptical of Jesus' powers. He did not say:

"Healing is impossible."

"There has to be another explanation."

"It must be a psychosomatic phenomenon—the power of suggestion."

"Those healings won't last."

"He is doing it just to draw attention to himself."

"That is too much sensationalism and emotionalism."

"If He really has the power to heal, why doesn't He heal everybody?"

The centurion, although in a status leadership role himself, did not take on any of those arrogant responses. Because of his attitude, he would soon discover the truth that God is a rewarder of those who seek Him.

The centurion had a need. His servant was "lying paralyzed at home, suffering great pain" (Matthew 8:6). Luke, written by the physician, gives us the doctor's analysis. The servant was "about to die" (Luke 7:2).

The centurion was not looking for healing for self-centered reasons; that is, that the servant might get up in order to work to meet the needs of his employer. No, the centurion's desire for healing was out of compassion for the servant. Luke gives us that clue—the servant "was dear to him" (Luke 7:2, RSV).

What a wonderful combination in this centurion—a supervisor with sensitivity, a boss with compassion, a leader with love. A person who knew well the chain-of-command approach, he could have had the "top dog" attitude and been cold, impersonal, and brutal with his servant. In fact, the idea of being military often carries with it the attitude of being indifferent and detached. Some military leaders prefer that image. At one time, Caesar apologized for feeling pity for a slave. But this centurion was not interested in becoming like a Caesar.

It takes humility to express faith openly. The centurion's humility is seen in several different ways:

1. He did not feel worthy enough to ask Jesus personally for the healing of his slave. He was a Gentile, and Jesus was a Jew. He was aware of the attitude of Jews toward the Gentiles. While Matthew records that the centurion came to Jesus entreating Him (Matthew 8:5), Luke tells us how he came to Jesus. He did not at first come personally on a one-to-one basis; he came through representatives. He asked some of the Jewish elders to approach Jesus.

The centurion may have thought he had not earned the right to be heard by such a person as Jesus. He certainly did not think he was worthy (Matthew 8:8). Surely we can understand that. Aren't there people to whom we don't feel significant enough to go, like the president of the company, the governor of the state, or the mayor of the city?

2. As Jesus was approaching the centurion's house, the centurion sent friends to meet Jesus (Luke 7:6). The centurion still did not think that his status was sufficient to approach Jesus.

3. The centurion confessed to Jesus, "Lord, I am not worthy for You to come under my roof" (Matthew 8:8). What a thing for a Roman military officer to say to a Jewish civilian in an occupied country! This centurion was an expert in the chain-of-command relationship. A private does not fraternize with a captain. A corporal does not spend time in the home of a general. That kind of rank crossing does not normally happen. The centurion was giving to Jesus recognition of rank; the same type of rank that his men would give to him. This centurion sensed the kind of authority in Jesus that would place himself in the rank of private. His military training would have compelled him to say he was not worthy for Jesus to come to his house.

The centurion then said something that caused Jesus to respond, "Truly I say to you, I have not found such great faith with anyone in Israel" (Matthew 8:10). The centurion said something that showed that his faith was in the authority of Jesus: "Just say the word, and my servant will be healed. For I, too, am a man under authority, with soldiers under me; and I say to this one, 'Go!' and he goes, and to another, 'Come!' and he comes, and to my slave, 'Do this!' and he does it" (Matthew 8:8, 9).

I spent eight years in active military service. During boot camp, I learned what it meant to hear commandments and to obey them. I learned the saying, "It is not for you to reason why, it is for you to do or die." I learned that there were only two major choices in the battlefield—do it or be prepared to die.

That centurion had lived in that kind of system. He would say a word, and people would respond immediately because of his superiority in position. Here, he transferred that type of authority to Jesus; he affirmed that Jesus had authority over nature. Jesus could say to nature, to a disease, "Be gone," and nature would have no choice. It would obey Jesus, who had the superior position. This is how the centurion saw Jesus. No wonder he called Him "Lord."

That is the kind of faith that Jesus had not yet encountered in Israel. Instead of seeing Jesus with that kind of authority, the people of Israel questioned Him, tested Him, tried to put Him on the spot, slandered Him, and tried to trick Him. After His first sermon in Nazareth, the people of Israel tried to kill Him. But this centurion rightly understood that Jesus was the God over nature who had come in flesh.

Jesus then said something to the centurion that every person today should never forget. Nor should this statement ever be taken out of the context of the faith of a man in the authority of Jesus. Jesus said many will come from the east and the west and be a part of the kingdom of Heaven, but those whom we most expect to be a part of the kingdom of Heaven—the religious ones—will be cast into outer darkness (Matthew 8:11, 12). In the context of this miracle, what would cause them to be cast out? It was lack of faith in the authority of Jesus.

Today, when we are reluctant to believe in the power of God when it might not conform to our understanding of science, our senses, or society's agenda, what can we learn from Jesus' statement? We have done something terrible today in the name of Christianity. We have come to believe that man can do anything that he desires to do, given enough technology and time, but God cannot. We have come close to teaching that God checked in His power at the end of the apostolic era, but the Bible does not affirm that.

Is it possible that we have caved in to the teaching that this world is controlled by naturalism? That is, everything that happens is done by natural laws and does not need any supernatural One over the laws. There is no such thing as natural laws. They are all supernatural. They were created by God, and God is still Lord over them. Consequently, He can do whatever He pleases. Nothing is impossible with God. He is not trapped inside nature's laws. He can and does intervene in His natural laws when He wants to. And He will not be outvoted, vetoed, or impeached for doing so. He does not need the Christians' majority vote to be powerful. We may be uncomfortable with that concept of God. If we are, it is probably because it violates our idolatry of science. It also violates our ego. If God is in that kind of control, we are not in the driver's seat.

As military men are to obey their officers on the battle line without question, all of nature obeys God without question. As a matter of a fact, the only parts of God's creation that have been given the ability and freedom to choose whether or not to obey God are man and the angels. The stars, the mountains, the seas, the wind, the trees, and the rest of nature do not have that option. Whenever God speaks to a tree, it has to obey. Whenever God speaks to the wind, it has to obey.

That is the reason Jesus could command the storm to stop and it stopped. That is why God could command the hungry lions not to eat Daniel and they didn't. That is why God could command a fish to swallow Jonah and then spit him up onto the beach and it obeyed. The Bible is clear on this. God has created a covenant with day and night, and He has made the laws that control earth and sky (Jeremiah 33:25). God gives a command to the earth, and the command is obeyed (Psalm 147:15).

Our faith in God today will be directly correlated with our understanding of His authority over all things. If we think that He does not have authority over events and nature, then our faith will be weakened. And if our faith is weakened, our prayers will be general and sporadic. What that centurion had, Jesus expects us to have if we are going to be a part of the kingdom of Heaven. When God expects faith from us today, He is not expecting that we push some special button inside of us that relates only to religious matters. Faith is a normal part of living; it is the sixth sense of humans. No one can live five minutes without exercising faith. The issue is not whether we do or do not have faith. What or who is the authority figure for our faith?

Faith is described as "the assurance of things hoped for, the conviction of things not seen" (Hebrews 11:1). Other translations say it this way:

> Now faith is the confident assurance of that for which we hope, a conviction of the reality of things we do not see (Weymouth).

> Now faith means that we have confidence of what we hope for (Moffat).

> Faith gives substance to our hopes, and makes us certain of realities we do not see (New English Bible).

> Now faith is the assurance (the confirmation, the title deed) of the things [we] hope for, being the proof of things [we] do not see, and the conviction of their reality—faith perceiving as real fact what is not revealed to the senses (Amplified).

A person cannot see the air he breathes (except in southern California) but continues to breathe with faith conviction of something he cannot see. How do you know that there is not something in the next breath of air that will kill you? The only way you could know that would be to capture that air, take it to a lab, and have it tested. Then you would have to have faith in the person who tested it. The way to bypass that is to test it yourself. Then you would have to have faith in the people who taught you how to do it accurately.

A person cannot take a drink of water without faith. How do you know there is not something in that water that will kill you? A person cannot eat at a restaurant without faith. How do you know what is going on in the kitchen? A person cannot get out of bed and put his feet on the floor, particularly if he is sleeping upstairs, without faith. How does he know that somebody hasn't sawed a hole through the floor so that when he steps out of bed he goes right through to the basement?

We make plans, act, react, and function all day long out of faith. When God asks us to have faith, He is asking us to relate to Him with the kind of trust principle that we give to the air, the water, meals, and gravity.

But God expects us to lift Him up above all of those other things. He is the God of gods and Lord of lords. He has authority over all things in Heaven and on earth.

Jesus had undeniable and undiluted faith in God. The reason that the centurion's faith in Jesus was effective is because Jesus had an unwavering faith in God. Jesus' eye of faith could see the invisible. Only the one who can see the invisible can believe in the impossible.

Jesus performed His miracles by faith in the power of God. God's power is the same yesterday, today, and tomorrow. If the world does not believe in the power of God and if the church does not, who will?

The world deserves to see Christians on a Heaven-bound journey with faith that is bigger than anything on this earth. The earth will pass away, but God is forever.

CHAPTER SEVEN

NOT BAD; JUST BUSY

Matthew 6:5-15

Bill, his wife Kathleen, and their daughter Carolyn had been looking forward to spending some time at Big Bear, a family mountain resort. There was not a cloud in the sky when they got into their airplane at the small California airport and started on their way.

Bill was a busy executive as well as a good and careful pilot. He no doubt had many things on his mind as he began to maneuver the airplane toward the resort. He was no doubt talking with his family, thinking about important decisions at work, and flying the airplane, of course. He was busy doing good things, important and appropriate things. But in his busyness, he neglected an essential thing; he strayed a bit off course.

It happened at 12:05 P.M. on a Sunday afternoon on a Labor Day weekend. Their small plane hit a Mexican airliner over a residential area in Cerritos, California, killing everyone on both planes and several people on the ground.

Bill had neglected an essential. Isn't it easy for all of us to get busy doing good, important, appropriate, nice, spiritual, serving-type things and neglect some essentials? If the devil cannot make us too bad, then he can make us too busy to deepen our relationship with God. It is easy to get too busy in our workaholic, rushaholic, goaholic, spendaholic lifestyles.

There is a difference between what is important and what is essential. My right arm is important and nice to have, but it is not essential to my existence. If I lose it, I can continue to live. But my heart is more than important; it is also essential. If I lose it, I am gone.

The apostle Paul said that the outer man is decaying. We all know about that, don't we? Yet the inner man is being renewed day by day (2 Corinthians 4:16). The daily renewal of the inner man is not just important, but also essential. Each of us needs to ask, "Is my inner person really being renewed day by day?" Communication with God—regular and a lot of it—is essential for the renewal of the inner person. God does not want the inner person to burn out while we journey Heavenward. Our inner selves will fizzle out if we don't stay close to God.

Prayer is closing the communication gap between us and God. It keeps the passageways open so the character of Jesus can be seen in us as we journey.

God desires our prayers. He said, "I was ready to answer my people's prayers, but they did not pray" (Isaiah 65:1, TEV). God is always ready to answer His people who pray. In fact, He gets upset when we look to the technology of our day for help rather than to Him—"Woe to those who go down to Egypt for help, and rely on horses, and trust in chariots because they are many, and in horsemen because they are very strong, but they do not look to the Holy One of Israel, nor seek the Lord" (Isaiah 31:1).

As a Father, God yearns to hear His children, "The Lord is pleased when good men pray" (Proverbs 15:8, TEV). Surely we who are parents understand the desire of the Heavenly Father to hear His kids talk with Him. Isn't it wonderful when our grown children call us on the telephone or drop in to visit with us? One of the things that pleases me most is when our children share something with me just because they want me to know. It is one thing to know something in their lives; it is quite another for them to *want* us to know. Pleasing God involves regularly praying to Him as our Father because we *want* to.

What hinders us from making prayer a priority today? Perhaps it is because we live in an activity-centered culture, not a meditative/prayer culture; consequently, it is easy to think that prayer is not an activity or work and thus not as important. But prayer is indeed work—hard work.

Or is it because our prayers have not always been answered the way we wanted them to and so we quit asking? Or perhaps it is because of our pride, our dependence on our being right? It is easy to think that if we have the doctrine down pat, we don't have to pray.

Or what about our emphasis on Bible reading? Is it taking the place of our praying? Do we think that if we spend enough time reading the Bible, we do not need to pray? Can you imagine what would happen if my wife sent me a love letter while I was away on a trip; but when I returned home, I would not spend time talking with her—instead I would read her love letter over and over again? *Two-way* communication with God is essential.

Or perhaps we misunderstand the nature of God. God is our Father and our Friend. How many of us could get by saying to a close friend, "You are my close friend, but I am going to put you on hold and not talk with you any more unless I am in some kind of trouble"?

Of course, many of us claim that we don't have enough time to pray. Let's be honest. We have plenty of time, but our time is prioritized elsewhere. If time were the problem, television would be one colossal failure. The problem is not having a strong enough desire or not being self-disciplined.

On one occasion, Jesus' disciples asked, "Teach us to pray." On another occasion, Jesus asked them a penetrating question, "Could you not watch with me for one hour?" The disciples did not know how to answer.

What would happen if every Christian would pray for at least an hour a day? It boggles the mind, doesn't it? But we probably feel the same way the disciples did. We would like to be able to pray to God for one hour; we determine to do so. But after we have shared all we have on our minds, only ten minutes has gone by. How can we possibly learn to pray for such a long period of time?

One of the finest ways to begin is where Jesus began with His disciples. When they asked Him to teach them to pray, He gave them the Model Prayer. I am not suggesting that He gave this prayer as a set outline or that this is the way we ought always to pray, but that it can serve as a guide to us as we are learning to have more significant communication with God.

This Model Prayer (Matthew 6:9-13) can help us learn to pray more specifically. We can take each word or phrase of the model prayer and meditate upon its meaning to each of us personally, think about it creatively, relate it to where we are spiritually and practically, and then talk to God about it. I will show you what I mean.

Father

Think about the various aspects of a good father-child relationship. Thank God for bringing us into His family through Jesus Christ. God did it on purpose; we are no accident. He has given us His sperma (Holy Spirit) and thus His very nature. Thank God for not aborting us or abandoning us or abusing us.

We can thank God for listening to us. There are times when I say I am listening to my children, but I am not really paying attention. We can be thankful God is not like that. We can thank God for staying awake while we sleep. We can thank God for forgiving us when we do wrong. He protects us. How many times has God protected you? Even sometimes when you didn't even know you were in danger. As a Father, He provides for us in so many different ways— can you think of them? What about our daily needs? What about daily guidance? What about the feeling of love and joy?

As our Father, He knows us and loves us. He hurts when we hurt. We can interrupt Him at any time. We need no appointments. As our Father, He wants only the best for us, and He knows what is best for us.

With these prayer thoughts, get very specific. Thank Him for the various ways He has forgiven you. How do you know His love each day? Make lists. In what specific ways has He protected you? In what ways does He guide you? Verbalize the specifics and then thank Him.

Our Father

Emphasize the *our*. No person is an island. We are not disconnected from others. We belong. It is at this point that we can thank God for the other brothers and sisters in the family of God who worship with us, teach us, encourage us, and enrich our lives.

When we take seriously the "ourness" of *our Father,* we realize that we are not to be isolated individualists. We must treat others the way we want them to treat us. We are to treat older men as fathers, older women as mothers, younger men and women as brothers and sisters—all in a loving family relationship. Lift up that family to God by name. Having trouble with a brother? Disappointed in a sister? Talk to God about it. Ask for His guidance and help. Thank God specifically for those people who have contributed to your spiritual life.

Who Art in Heaven

Picture God on the throne and all that that means. He is in control. He sees everything from Heaven's perspective. Be specific about the issues you are dealing with and the situations that you are involved in, asking Him to reveal His perspective to you.

He is preparing a place for us in Heaven. Thank Him for planning to return to us, for allowing us to participate in eternal life when we don't deserve it, for loving us enough to protect us on Judgment Day.

He is in Heaven and is eternal. He is not a passing vapor. He is stable and secure for always and always. Be thankful that He is above time and space and is patient; He is not trapped by our environment. He is vast. He cannot be bound in anyone's boxes. Be thankful He is so big. Be thankful He is so adequate and so far above anything we can even imagine.

Hallowed Be Thy Name

Hallowed refers to respect and honor. The finest way we can honor someone is to imitate him. Think of all the characteristics of God you can, meditate upon them, thank Him, and then ask Him to help you live out those characteristics in your life. Be specific about situations in which you know you need a certain characteristic but as yet have not been able to show. God is loving, patient, understanding, forgiving, and faithful—these are characteristics we want to have in our characters.

Then think of the characteristics of God that we cannot imitate—those that are so high above us, that engender awe and reverence within us. He is omniscient, omnipresent, all-powerful, eternal, invisible, Lord (ruler), and Savior. Then express your respect and honor of Him.

Thy Will Be Done

Meditate upon what you know so far is God's will for you. Then ask specifically that He reveal His will to you as guidance in specific areas of your personal life—your inner person, your family, your church, your work, and your friendships—your particular situations. Ask that God help you to be willing to put His will into action.

Meditate upon what you know is God's will for your church, community, and nation. Then pray for your church. Pray for your community. Pray for the nation. Pray for specific needs that you know of on the mission fields. Pray concerning the ills of society—pornography, abortion, homosexuality, drug/alcohol abuse, violence. Ask God to bring the nation to repentance so His will can be done.

Give Us Our Daily Bread

It is not wrong to pray for material things, as long as our motivations are pure. And we need to remember the "our" aspect. Our prayers must move beyond our own personal needs. We are also to intercede for others. It would be good to keep a notebook of people and their needs as you find out about them; then you could remember to pray specifically for them—some of them daily, some weekly, and some monthly. If we truly want to grow and bear fruit, we must pray for others. Samuel said, "Far be it from me that I should sin against the Lord by ceasing to pray for you." (1 Samuel 12:23).

Forgive Us As We Forgive Others

This is the time to deal with your sins. This is the time to bring before the Lord your hurts, disappointments, and fears. Ask forgiveness, and ask Him to enable you to forgive. Then leave the hurt and burden with Him. Has someone hurt you? Don't nurse it, rehearse it, curse it, or research it, but disperse it to God—He can reverse it.

Confess specifically your personal sins. Be honest. Don't try to hide them, excuse them, or rationalize them.

Lay prostrate before Him if need be. Then experience His forgiveness and thank Him.

Lead Us Not Into Temptation But Deliver Us From Evil

As long as we live in this world, we will be tempted. The temptations are different for each individual and change at various stages of our lives. Talk to God specifically about the areas that bother you. Ask for His guidance and understanding. Call upon Him for the strength you need to resist. Ask for protection from Satan's devices. Ask Him to reveal the ways of escape that He has for you. Thank Him for understanding the temptations you face.

For Thine Is the Kingdom, the Power, and the Glory Forever

This is the time for praise. Praise Him for all that He does and is. This is the time for worship.

Yes, it is possible to pray for long periods. It takes thought and effort—and a lot of desire and commitment. Yes, we can do it. We can get up an hour earlier or go to bed an hour later. We can turn off the television and go to a quiet place for an hour. We can use our driving time or the time we are standing in lines or waiting in offices.

And yes, the Lord has taught us to pray. Perhaps one day He can say, "Thank you for watching with Me one hour."

CHAPTER EIGHT

GRATITUDE THAT GAINS ALTITUDE

Luke 17:11-19

It's not just *where* we are journeying, but *how* we are journeying that matters. What is our attitude as we journey along the narrow way?

Andy was born with many handicaps and disadvantages. He was born with one eye, no arms, and no legs. Instead of feet, he had a couple of flippers attached to his torso. When Andy's parents saw him, they did not want him. He remained in hospitals as an unwanted boy until he was ten years old; then Leonard and Hazel adopted him. Today, Andy is a college graduate, can drive a car, writes music, and does many things that the average person can do.

Another boy was born. He also began life with many disadvantages. His mother showed him no affection and no discipline. He failed academically in school and dropped out of high school during his junior year. He joined the Marines but was court-martialed. He went to a foreign country and married. But his wife continually belittled him, demanded more than he could give, and even locked him in the bathroom at times for punishment.

Estranged from his wife and back in the United States, feeling inferior and different from others, he arose one morning and took a rifle to the place where he worked. There, from a sixth floor window, he shot and killed President John F. Kennedy, and wounded Texas Governor John Connally.

Both boys were disadvantaged. One gave to life, and the other took a life. One was grateful for the little he did have, the other was not. In spite of being rejected, in spite of his many deformities, Andy once said, "I would describe life as a never-ending road with its bumps and smoothness. Once I came to a bump of sadness where I thought life was not worth living. But as usual, I carried on. Now I have come a long, long way on the road to freedom."

Andy saw his handicaps and decided to develop his potentials. Lee Harvey Oswald saw his handicaps and decided to lash out and destroy.

Do you ever feel like life has handed you too many raw deals? Disappointments? Setbacks? That there is not much to be thankful for but much reason to be hateful?

Being thankful is not always easy. In fact, the Bible calls it a sacrifice (Psalm 50:14, 23; 51:17; 54:6). How can the giving of thanks be a sacrifice? Isn't sacrifice the giving up of something we value, something we want? It certainly is. And so is the giving of thanks. When we give thanks, we have to give up a bit of our ego. Giving thanks is giving up something we want—our independence.

A person cannot be thankful without admitting dependency. Gratitude is an admission that without God and others, we cannot make it. Who among us can cause the sun to shine? We are needy. Who among us can cause rain to fall? We are needy. Who among us by himself can plant, cultivate, harvest, and process soybeans into the many products made from them? We are needy. Who among us can eradicate diphtheria, polio, measles, and small pox? We are needy.

But isn't that easy to forget? There seems to be a paradox among us—the less we have, the easier it is to be thankful. When abundance comes, sometimes the attitude of thankfulness is forgotten.

I was reared in southern Illinois. We had a heating stove in only one room of the house. I never knew that some people got out of bed in the morning to a warm house. I was thankful for those few times when the fire didn't go out and the house was warm in the morning. Do you think I am consciously thankful for that now? Isn't it easy to forget when the extraordinary becomes the ordinary?

We had a well in the back yard for our water supply and an outhouse nearly a half block away. I was thankful when I didn't have to go out in the snow to draw water or to do you-know-what. Do you think I am consciously thankful for indoor plumbing today?

Gratefulness is more than an inner feeling or an attitude. After all, impression without expression leads to depression. Gratefulness is not just a delight in the heart, but also a doing with the hands. It is not just sentimentalism; it is also service. It is not just a feeling; it is also a function. It is not just thanks*giving,* but also thanks*living.*

True thankfulness always motivates us to do something to express it.

She was there, but she was lonely. When she went home, she went to an empty house with no one to hold her or put a log on the fire. But she was there amid the high and the mighty and walked along with them. When her time came, she dropped in the two smallest coins. They were all she had. We call them the widow's mites.

If anyone knew what she had done, he might have thought, "What irresponsibility!" But Jesus was there, and He knew. And He thought, "What a grateful attitude."

She slipped into the room. She was unwanted, for she was from the wrong side of the tracks and had the wrong kind of life-style. The house was filled with the social elite, but it was an "open house"; so they could not refuse her entrance.

She had a purpose in coming. She brought a jar filled with perfume, worth the equivalent of a year's salary. She broke the jar and spilled it all on Him. It was probably her life's savings. The people in the house must have thought, "What a waste!" But Jesus thought, "What a grateful attitude."

Thanksgiving will turn us around from the busy, fast-lane world. It will slow us down enough to express our thanks. And with thanksgiving there comes healing—healing of the whole self. It will help get rid of greed, selfishness, envy, and jealousy. It will heal our inner attitudes and spirit.

The village is unknown, and the names of the lepers are not recorded, but what happened that day is a lesson for all of us. Ten leprous men were sticking together. They were no doubt together because they were the only ones who could accept each other. Leprosy was a disease that made a person a social outcast. They were required by law to keep their distance from others. A leper would have to yell out, "Unclean," whenever there were other people around. Wouldn't that be a degrading thing to have to do?

But individuals cannot stay aloof from others all the time. People need people, and no one needs people more than those who are forced to be kept at even more than an arm's length in distance. These ten lepers were together in their common misery. Isn't it true that when we are in pain, we learn how much we need one another.

These lepers were staying close to each other but stood at a distance from others (Luke 17:12). When they saw Jesus, they raised their voices with the request, "Have mercy on us!"

These ten lepers saw in Jesus something different, and what Jesus heard was unique. Instead of hearing, "Unclean, unclean," which would have signaled for Him to stay away, He heard the words, "Have mercy," which signaled, "Come closer to us."

Jesus looked upon them. He must have seen open sores, fingers and noses gone or partly gone. He would have seen grotesque, repulsive-looking creatures—if He saw them as others saw them. But Jesus always looked beyond the problems. He saw people with needs. He saw people through eyes of love.

Isn't that what we need to do? Sometimes we allow people's problems to prevent us from seeing the people with pain.

Jesus' response was no doubt unexpected by these men. They probably expected Him to do something for them. Instead, He asked them to do something. "Go and show yourself to the priest."

That would have sounded a bit premature, for lepers would show themselves to the priest after being healed in order to have their healing validated. These men were to go while still diseased.

These lepers did not do what many of us might do. They did not scornfully say, "What good will that do? It does no good to be seen in our diseased state; if we go like this, the priest will further confirm what we know—that we are lepers."

They did not criticize or question. They did not ask for another program; they simply obeyed. Because of their obedience out of faith, they were cleansed of their leprosy on the way to the priest. However, they had to be officially pronounced clean by the priest before they could function in society without the stigma of being unclean.

Luke told this episode, not so much to show the power of Jesus, but to show the importance of gratitude. Out of the ten lepers who were healed, only one returned. Instead of rushing to see the priest to be officially pronounced clean and to get on with life, he took time to return to thank the Great Physician. Part of the problem of our ungratefulness today is that we do not slow down and take time to turn to people who have helped us with our expressions of gratitude. We want to get on with life—and in the fast lane. This is especially true for those who feel they have been denied a full life for some reason or another for a long time.

I recently had a heart attack and spent a week in an intensive care unit in a hospital. I could not wait to get out of there and get on with living. I can understand those lepers' wanting to get to the priest as fast as possible.

But one man delayed his own selfish desires and turned back to express his appreciation to Jesus. Not only did he take, but he also gave. He took the healing, and he gave proper credit. He glorified God with a loud voice (Luke 17:15). As he had used a loud voice to make the request for mercy, he used that voice in the same intensity to give thanks. As he was not ashamed to ask publicly for help, and he was not ashamed to give public credit to the One who had helped him.

When we are in severe need, we are driven at times to ask publicly for help—such as the emergency ward of the hospital. But sometimes we forget to return to express our appreciation of those who helped.

When I got out of the hospital after my heart attack, I wrote the hospital administrator a letter of appreciation, praising by name the doctors and nurses who had helped me and treated me so well. But prior to that, I continually thanked and glorified God. As I lay in the hospital bed with tubes in me and all sorts of monitoring equipment around me, I could not help but praise God for being a fantastic Creator and for giving man the creative ability to design and build the equipment that could help keep me alive and on the way to healing.

We must not neglect to thank God for the many ways He blesses us. One of the reasons we set aside one day of the week is to thank God through worship.

There is a direct relationship between humility and thanksgiving. The leper not only gave thanks to Jesus, but "fell on his face at His feet" (Luke 17:16).

There are several aspects of thanksgiving that we find here—take time, be willing to detour your plans, thank God first, don't be ashamed to give public testimony to God's involvement in your life, become humble, and literally give thanks to God.

One of the astounding facts about this whole episode is in the identity of the man who gave the thanks. While nine might be called "true blue" Jews, the one that returned to give thanks was a Samaritan. A Samaritan was a bi-racial— really a multi-racial—person. He was part Jew and part Gentile. The prejudices went back hundreds of years and were deeply entrenched in their hearts.

Jews and Samaritans were geographically, religiously, and socially detached from one another. Religiously, the Samaritans worshiped in a different place, accepted only the first five books of the Old Testament, and looked for a different kind of Messiah than the Jews.

Socially, they would not mix with each other in usual situations. In fact, an orthodox Jew traveling from Galilee to Jerusalem or vice versa would not even go through Samaria, which is the territory between the two. An orthodox Jew in Jerusalem would go east, cross the Jordan River, go north on the desert side, until the Samaritan territory was passed, and then turn back west, recross the river, and enter into Galilee. If a Jew did put his foot on Samaritan soil, he would shake the dust off his feet and declare himself religiously unclean. The prejudices were so deep that one of the slanderous comments made about Jesus by Jewish Pharisees was that Jesus was a Samaritan.

It was interesting that while these ten shared a common misery, they stayed together. But when the Samaritan turned back, the other nine did not turn back with him. It may be possible that since they were cleansed, they suddenly wanted nothing else to do with this Samaritan. The common element that had drawn them together—leprosy—was no longer there. In fact, the other nine may have been glad to see the Samaritan depart from them.

Isn't it interesting that, at times, it is the most unlikely ones who seem to be most grateful? Sometimes, brand new Christians who have not had a history of tasting of the benefits of God seem to be more thankful than leaders in the church who have received the benefits of God in the fellowship of His people for years. Sometimes, those who seem to be more religious have the attitude that they deserve to receive God's benefits.

Here is a foreigner who models what it means to be grateful. In the previous chapter, we learned of foreigner who modeled what it means to have real faith in the unlimited authority of Jesus. Now, again, it is a foreigner who provides a worthy example.

When Jesus saw the Samaritan coming to Him and heard him give thanks, Jesus asked, "Were there not ten cleansed? But the nine—where are they?" (Luke 17:17). Perhaps Jesus is asking us that question: "Where are you?" It may be that our answer is, "We are busy. We are getting involved again. We are active. We are attending meetings. We are making money. We are involved with family activities. We are taking some needed time off."

But when Jesus asks, "Where are you?" He is asking, "Where is your appreciation?"

While the other nine were cleansed of leprosy, this man's gratitude and faith expressed in that gratitude made him "well" (Luke 17:19). What is the difference between being cleansed (Luke 17:14) and being made well? A person can be cleansed of a disease but not be well in his relationships. A person can be cleansed physically but not be well socially and spiritually. This one Samaritan gained far more than freedom from leprosy.

Is it possible that he returned and thanked Jesus because that was his characteristic prior to being cleansed? Is it possible that he was the kind of person who looked for the positive amid the negative? While he had leprosy (as did the other nine), he still saw much in life for which to be thankful. He could be thankful for the ability to see, to hear, to talk, to be able walk, and to have friends.

Is it possible that the other nine saw life in a negative way? When they were healed, they continued to be negative and complaining for all the years that they had been out of society.

It is interesting that Jesus did not command these ten to return to give thanks. His command was only to go and show themselves to the priest. So the other nine were indeed obeying His command. But they did not have gratitude with their obedience.

Real gratitude can never be commanded. A person who expresses thanks because he is told to—"Say, 'Thank you'"—is a person who may say the outer syllables but not have the inner sincerity. Real gratitude comes from our inner response to life. It is unrehearsed. It is never a rote obedience to a command.

There is another reason this Samaritan could have been thankful. While having fellowship with the Jews because of leprosy, he may have changed religions. Otherwise, there would have been no reason to have shown himself to the priest. In fact, a Jewish priest would not have been interested in the Samaritan's coming to him.

Tragedy in the life of the Samaritan may very well have brought triumph in his relationship to God. Apparently, tragedy brought him to the truth; catastrophe brought him to Christ. A hurtful situation brought him to the helpful person.

That same thing happens again and again today. When the temporary problems (and all of them are temporary) bring us to the eternal person of Jesus—when earthly setbacks bring us to the Savior—indeed, there is reason to turn back, glorify God, fall on our faces, and thank Jesus. And not only for the healing, but also for the circumstances that brought us to the place to seek Him and to cry out, "Have mercy on us."

There is an underlying truth in this episode that Christians today must grow into. Our relationship to God and His Son Jesus, our activities for Him, and our responses to Him must not come out of guilt feelings, but rather out of gratitude. God wants our activities, our services, and our gifts to be expressions of gratitude for what He has done, not responses of guilt as we try to cover up our past. Many people have become spiritual workaholics out of guilt. That does not free them; it fetters them. It will not better them, but may eventually embitter them.

It is gratitude, not guilt, that frees us to delightful actions.

It is gratitude that prompted an old man to visit an old broken pier on the eastern seacoast of Florida. Every Friday night, until his death in 1973, he would return, walking slowly and slightly stooped with a large bucket of shrimp. The sea gulls would flock to this old man, and he would feed them from his bucket.

Many years before, in October, 1942, Captain Eddie Rickenbacker was on a mission in a B-17 to deliver an important message to General Douglas MacArthur in New Guinea.

But there was an unexpected detour which would hurl Captain Eddie into the most harrowing adventure of his life.

Somewhere over the South Pacific the Flying Fortress became lost beyond the reach of radio. Fuel ran dangerously low, so the men ditched their plane in the ocean....

For nearly a month Captain Eddie and his companions would fight the water, and the weather, and the scorching sun.

They spent many sleepless nights recoiling as giant sharks rammed their rafts. The largest raft was nine by five. The biggest shark ... ten feet long.

But of all their enemies at sea, one proved most formidable: starvation. Eight days out, their rations were long gone or destroyed by the salt water. It would take a miracle to sustain them. And a miracle occurred.

In Captain Eddie's own words, "Cherry," that was the B-17 pilot, Captain William Cherry, "read the service that afternoon, and we finished with a prayer for deliverance and a hymn of praise. There was some talk, but it tapered off in the oppressive heat. With my hat pulled down over my eyes to keep out some of glare, I dozed off."

Now this is still Captain Rickenbacker talking ... "Something landed on my head. I knew that it was a sea gull. I don't know how I knew, I just knew.

"Everyone else knew too. No one said a word, but peering out from under my hat brim without moving my head, I could see the expression on their faces. They were staring at that gull. The gull meant food ... if I could catch it."

And the rest, as they say, is history.

Captain Eddie caught the gull. Its flesh was eaten. Its intestines were used for bait to catch fish. The survivors were sustained and their hopes renewed because a lone sea gull, uncharacteristically hundreds of miles from land, offered itself as a sacrifice.

You know that Captain Eddie made it.

And now you also know ... that he never forgot.

Because every Friday evening, about sunset ... on a lonely stretch along the eastern Florida seacoast ... you could see an old man walking ... white-haired, bushy-eyebrowed, slightly bent.

His bucket filled with shrimp was to feed the gulls ... to remember that one which, on a day long past, gave itself without a struggle ... like manna in the wilderness.[1]

Eddie Rickenbacker fed the sea gulls—out of gratitude to a sea gull that had saved his life.

Gratitude is an essential attitude for our Heaven-bound journey. Let's fill our buckets and offer them to God in gratitude.

---

[1] Excerpt from "The Old Man and the Gulls" from *Paul Harvey's The Rest of the Story* by Paul Aurandt. Copyright ©1977 by Paulynne, Inc. Reprinted by permission of Doubleday, a division of Bantam, Doubleday, Dell Publishing Group, inc.

CHAPTER NINE

WHAT ARE YOU DOING ON THE WAY?

Luke 10:25-37

There are some things in life that are hard to understand.
Why is butter so hard when the bread is so soft?
While Jesus could turn stones into bread, why is it some restaurants can turn bread into stone?
How do discounts end up costing so much?
Why is your car worth so little when you trade it in, and so much when the car lot sells it?
How can the same store have a going-out-of-business sale so often?
How come the guys who marry our daughters are never good enough, but still our grandchildren are the greatest in the world?
How come such good looking people can look so terrible in the photos on their driver's licenses?
There are also some things that must be difficult for Heaven to understand.
How can people love God so much and yet love people so little?
How can Christians give God so much time in religious meetings, but give hurting people so little time when those meetings are over?
How can Christians sometimes get caught up in legalism rather than love?
How can branches be connected to the Vine—Jesus (who was so involved with people)—while the fruit can so isolated from people?

Jesus was getting at those kind of contradictions with His illustration of the Good Samaritan.

I recently saw a couple of bumper stickers that illustrate something of Jesus' concern. One said, "Caution, I drive the way you do." What if everybody drove the way I do? What if God said, "Caution, I love the way you do"?

The other was a combination of two bumper stickers. The one on the left said, "I love Jesus." The one on the right said, "I love to get even." Apparently, the owner of the car did not understand that those two were contradictory. But isn't that the way we are sometimes? We can divorce our love for Jesus from our actions and reactions.

That seemed to be a part of the problem of the lawyer who approached Jesus with an important question: "Teacher, what shall I do to inherit eternal life?" (Luke 10:25).

A Jewish lawyer was different from the lawyers we know today. He was a Biblical scholar—a theologian. He would be more like a seminary professor of our time. He was an expert in the Jewish law and a teacher of its interpretations.

However, this scholar did not ask that question in order to be challenged by Jesus to change his priorities and practices. He asked in order to test Jesus. He was playing theological chess with Jesus for the purpose of trying to checkmate Him.

Isn't that easy to do with one another today? In fact, it is easy to do with God as well. We often raise questions about the Biblical text and assume we know more about the situation than did the Holy Spirit who inspired the text.

However, Jesus would not be trapped by this scholar. He would not play his games. Jesus threw the question back at him so he could take the responsibility for its answer. "What is written in the Law? How does it read to you?" (Luke 10:26).

Notice the balance Jesus brings. The scholar asked, "What shall I *do?*" It was a question that dealt with behavior. But Jesus replied by connecting behavior to God's law. It is not enough just to do: we also must know. It is not enough to have fruitage: we must also must have rootage. Jesus brought him back to the basis for his ethical decisions—what God has written.

Isn't it interesting that when the scholar asked about how to get eternal life, Jesus did not answer with a simple, pat procedure such as the four spiritual laws or a set plan of salvation? Before giving any answer, Jesus wanted to hear this man's understanding.

The scholar must have enjoyed answering Jesus' question. If anyone knew about the Law, it would have been this man. He had no hesitancy in quoting from memory, and what he quoted was an excellent answer (Luke 10:27). His quote combined the truth of Deuteronomy 6:5 and Leviticus 19:18. It lined up with Jesus' own evaluation of what the greatest commandment is (Matthew 22:36-40). He was journeying in the right direction.

Jesus liked the man's answer. "You have answered correctly," He said. But Jesus added something to his answer, "Do this and you will live" (Luke 10:28). In a similar situation, Jesus replied, "You are not far from the kingdom of God" (Mark 12:34). When Jesus said, "You are not far," He meant, "You are not far away from inheriting eternal life because you have adequate knowledge."

But He was not saying, "You have arrived." Although the man's answer indicated that he was not far away, it also indicated he had not gone far enough. Knowledge must be followed up with doing. Memory of the text must be followed up with an application of its truth. Belief must be backed up with behavior. Jesus knew that this man must move from hearing to helping, from devotion to deeds, from thinking to doing, from intellectualizing to involvement, from the mental to movement, from being correct in understanding to being compassionate in undertakings—in short, from being a scholar to being a servant.

That's why Jesus moved from what the person was reading to what he was doing.

The scholar did not mind that answer because he was accustomed to dodging personal responsibility by raising complex theological questions. This scholar liked to stay in the realm of discussion rather than move into the arena of doing. He wanted to stick with philosophy rather than practice, with speculation rather than service, with talk rather than walk. He wanted to stay in the schoolroom atmosphere and bat around questions and answers rather than be in the streets where people were being battered. So he responded with the philosophical question, "Who is my neighbor?" (Luke 10:29).

The scholar was looking for Jesus to philosophize. But Jesus did not cave in to what he wanted. Jesus' response showed that God's understanding of love is simple, not complex. It is practical, not philosophical. God's concept of love cuts immediately through a long discussion and gets to the practicalities of everyday life—with friends, beggars, employees, peddlers, servants, and all the rest.

Jesus turned the question around. Jesus was not concerned that he identify who would be a neighbor to *him,* but rather to whom he would be a neighbor. What does it mean to be neighborly?

Thus Jesus answered the philosophical question with a practical parable. A parable is an earthly illustration that clarifies and applies an eternal truth. The point is, being neighborly is to be like the man in this story.

The scholar had replied that we are to love God and love our neighbors as ourselves. That is correct. That is the balance of love.

Jesus' parable made it clear that if we really love God, we will take the risk to love others. If we really love ourselves, we will not have to protect self by failing to take the risk to make time and monetary investments in others.

The parable is tender but tough. It is tender because it affirms the compassion of one man, but tough because it suggests that if we do not adopt this life-style, we may not inherit eternal life.

At first, the parable sounds simple—just help a person in need. But a closer examination shows that though simple in concept and language, the tradition-shattering truths contained within it are hard to take.

"A certain man was going down from Jerusalem to Jericho; and he fell among robbers, and they stripped him and beat him, and went off leaving him half dead" (Luke 10:30). Presumably, this man was a Jew; otherwise, at this time in history, the priest and Levite would not have been expected to stop and help because of their deep prejudices. It is interesting that no name is given to this man and no status is ascribed to him. It appears that he was an unknown, a "nobody." Perhaps both the priest and Levite would have stopped if the man had been recognizable. They would probably had stopped if he had been a man of influence—like a banker, a doctor, or a politician.

Isn't it easier to reach out to help others when we know that they may be in a position to repay us? But a nobody whom we may never see again? That is a different story.

The road from Jerusalem to Jericho was narrow and winding, providing many hiding places for robbers. It was known by the people in that area as being quite treacherous, especially for lone travelers.

"By chance a certain priest was going down on that road" (Luke 10:31). Many of the opportunities that we have to help someone come to us "by chance." We do not anticipate it, plan for it, or make provisions to help. We have not put it on our calendars. Of course, there are opportunities to help that we can plan for. It is the "by chance" opportunities, however, that test our compassion and priorities.

The fact that the priest was going *down* indicates that he was going away from Jerusalem (descending in altitude). He was a member of what we today might call the "clergy," and he had evidently been to Jerusalem to fulfill his professional responsibilities. Now he was on the way home. He had been involved in the ritualistic sacrifices, but he was not going to make personal sacrifice on this road. It is one thing to pass up someone we do not see, but it is quite another to see someone and pass them up on purpose. This priest saw him, but "he passed by on the other side" (Luke 10:31).

His neglect was intentional; he purposely stayed at a distance. He did not want to get close enough even to hear a cry for help. Few of us really want to get close to someone else's misery, for to do so is the first step in expressing brotherly love. What we see becomes the first step to what we do with our hands—or pocketbooks. If we close our eyes or turn the other way, we can more easily "pass by on the other side." This priest may have seen the man briefly and then quickly turned away his eyes and crossed to the other side to give the impression that he had never seen the hurting man. He was trying to fool everyone. He was not doing what he should have been on his journey.

85

We can surely identify with him and remember times when we have done the same thing. But we know that we cannot fool God. He sees when we pass by on the other side. Jesus knows of our purposeful neglect, and He takes it seriously. He takes it personally.

He said, "I was hungry, and you gave Me nothing to eat; I was thirsty, and you gave Me nothing to drink; I was a stranger, and you did not invite Me in; naked, and you did not clothe Me; sick, and in prison, and you did not visit Me" (Matthew 25:42, 43).

And the people answered, "When did we see *You* like that?" The implication is that if they had seen *Jesus,* they would have stopped and done something—but they didn't see *Jesus.* They just saw some ordinary nobodies.

Jesus replied, "To the extent that you did not do it to one of the least of the these, you did not do it to Me" (Matthew 25:45). Jesus expects that if we can say, "I love God and my neighbor," we should be demonstrating that love. Love to our neighbors is an outgrowth—a fruit—of our love to God. And our love to God always has love to others as its expressional goal.

Then a professional religious staff member, a Levite, also came, saw, and passed by on the other side. When we become so hooked on our institutional responsibilities that we pass by with indifference and as if we are nearsighted, we become like the Levite. The Pharisees were so concerned about their traditions that they criticized Jesus when He reached out to the needs of hurting people in ways that violated their ritualistic ways.

Would we stop and help someone if doing so would make us late to a religious service? It's not always where you are going that's important. What are you doing on the way?

The priest and the Levite probably had rationalizations that soothed their consciences:

1. I have been away from home quite a while performing religious duties; my family is expecting me home soon.
2. I am tired.
3. I have an appointment.
4. Somebody who has more time will stop and help.
5. He might be a decoy, and I might get hurt or robbed if I stop and help.

Can't you imagine the thoughts of the hurting man as he saw religious leaders coming by (assuming he recognized who they were):

"Thank God, somebody that is committed to God is drawing near. He will surely stop and help me. There is somebody coming whom I can trust—one of God's religious leaders. He will understand. He will take the time to help."

The question, "Who is my neighbor?" is about to be answered. Sometimes the people who need help and the people who can give help have opposite views about the meaning of the word *neighbor*.

The story reached a turning point when a "certain Samaritan" came by. He also saw the hurting man, but he did not go by. He felt compassion. He got close, not as a spectator, but as a helper.

But he was the wrong kind of person to help a Jew—he was from the wrong race, he was not a member of the community, he was an outsider. He knew that Jews hated Samaritans and that prejudices ran deep. But somehow a man in need at that moment was bigger than the prejudices of lifetime. The Samaritan could have thought:

1. To help this Jew is to help a cause that is competitive against my people.
2. To help this Jew is to help someone stay alive who perpetuates hatred against my people.
3. To help this Jew is to save someone who is different religiously from me.
4. To help this Jew is to take money away from my own people.
5. To help this Jew is to help someone who may not show any appreciation toward me.

But none of those thoughts were viable to this Samaritan, and they should not become issues in our service for others today. I read not long ago in a nondenominational journal an article concerning giving missionary funds to help people in other countries who do not belong to the fellowship of the giver. This article opposed the practice because to do so would be to help people who could not benefit that fellowship. Such an attitude is not Christlike. Such an attitude is the opposite of the attitude of the Samaritan, whom Jesus praised through His parable.

The Samaritan took several risks:

1. He stopped in an area where robbers were active.
2. He used his own oil and wine to bind up the wounds. Oil and wine were used medicinally in that day. To use them up might mean that he would not have any left in case he would get sick on the journey.
3. He not only bound the man's wound's, but also put him on his own beast and let the man travel a distance with him.
4. He paid the innkeeper the equivalent of two-day's wages (two denarii). That would be like spending $100 or more for someone today.
5. He promised the innkeeper that whatever was spent beyond that sum of money, he would pay it later. In other words, he was saying, "Put that on my bill."

We can see from this example that compassion may be costly; love can be extravagant; love can be, and usually is, risk-taking. This Samaritan demonstrated what Paul meant when he said, "Owe no one anything but love." In other words, love is a debt we owe other people that is never to be stamped, "Paid in full."

Jesus then asked the scholar the practical question, "Which one of these three do you think proved to be a neighbor to the man who fell into robbers' hands?" (Luke 10:36). He turned the scholar's thoughts from being inward-oriented to being outward-oriented. The scholar understood clearly Jesus' illustration and answered, "The one who showed mercy toward him" (Luke 10:37).

Jesus then connected the initial question of the scholar to the answer. The initial question was, "What shall I do?" And Jesus replied, "Go and do the same."

Jesus moved this question-and-answer from speculation to service—from philosophy to practice. And anyone who is reading this will miss the point if he does not move beyond the principle of this parable to the practice of it—"Go and do the same."

It is one thing to become a scholar of theological issues, such as the virgin birth, the millennium, miracles, and many others. To know Jesus, however, involves learning from Him what is to be our practical reaction toward the hungry, the distressed, the hurting, and the neglected people around us. To love the way Jesus loved is not asking, "Who will be *my* neighbor?" but, "Who is needing help from me?"

To love as the Samaritan did is to love as Jesus does. It includes at least the following:

1. Keep our eyes open to see the hurting around us.
2. Do not turn away quickly and pretend that we have not seen.
3. Do not cross on the other side of the street. Be available.
4. Be willing to have our plans interrupted.
5. Be willing to improvise. Be creative.
6. Be flexible and adaptable.
7. Let our help to others rise above our prejudices.
8. Don't restrict our help to only those in "our" group. Be inclusive.
9. Don't allow spiritual rituals to eliminate social responsibilities. Be open.
10. Don't restrict our neighbors to those we know.
11. Don't restrict our neighbors to those who are like us.
12. Don't restrict our neighbors to those who can return the favor. Be selfless.
13. Being neighborly involves the ability to pass by but the commitment not to do so.
14. Being neighborly is being Christlike. To be a neighbor is to be a Christian.

Jesus was like the Good Samaritan. No one was more "religious" than Jesus. Yet no one was more helpful to people's needs than He. Being helpful to others is a part of Heaven-bound living.

During World War II, bombs fell in the area of a small village that had a statue of Jesus. The statue of Jesus with His arms outstretched was broken into several small pieces. After the war, the citizens of the area decided to reconstruct that statue. But the hands could not be located. Some people suggested that a brand new statue be constructed. But they decided to keep the handless statue of Jesus standing.

Today at the base of that statue of Jesus with arms outstretched but with no hands are these words:

I have no hands but your hands to do my work today. I have no feet but your feet to lead men on the way. I have no tongue but your tongue to tell men how I died. I have no help but your help to bring men to God's side.

Walking with Jesus involves being Jesus' helping hands along our way.

Then the King will say to those on His right, "Come, you who are blessed of My Father, inherit the kingdom prepared for you from the foundation of the world. For I was hungry, and you gave Me something to eat; I was thirsty, and you gave Me drink; I was a stranger, and you invited Me in; naked, and you clothed Me; I was sick, and you visited Me; I was in prison, and you came to Me." Then the righteous will answer Him, saying, "Lord, when did we see You hungry, and feed you or thirsty, and give You drink? And when did we see You, a stranger, and invite You in, or naked, and clothe You? And when did we see You sick, or in prison, and come to You?" And the King will answer and say to them, "Truly I say to you, to the extent that you did it to one of these brothers of Mine, even the least of them, you did it to Me" (Matthew 25:34-40).

CHAPTER TEN

NO PAIN, NO GAIN

Matthew 27:32; 28:7

It was Sunday, October 16, 1949. The time: 6:00 A.M. A high-school sophomore woke up and looked out his upstairs bedroom window. His father was picking up some odds and ends that he (the son) had left in the backyard the day before. Feeling guilty that he had not put those things away himself, he yelled out the window, "Hey, Dad, just leave those there. I'll pick them up."

Then he dozed off for a while longer. (All of us have been there, haven't we? We are awake but not quite ready to get up, and we feel good about being able to sleep a while longer. It's like being able to cheat on time.) But then it happened. The boy opened his eyes suddenly. Was it a dream? Then he heard it again. His mother was screaming. The stairway had never been shorter as he flew down to the living room. His dad was sitting in the living room chair, but was motionless.

The son took his dad's pulse; it was very weak. But while the boy kept his finger on the pulse-point, the pulse stopped. My dad was dead.

I was there when the doctor came to the house and said, "He's gone." I was there when the funeral director came. I stood paralyzed as they took the covered body to the waiting black hearse. I later stood with Mother as we selected the casket and made the arrangements. I stood at the open casket following the funeral. I was there when they lowered the casket into the ground.

There was no doubt about it. It was not imaginary. Glennon H. Staton was dead. No one has ever seen him since—that is, no one here on earth.

There was no doubt about it. It was not imaginary. Jesus was dead. The evidence was overwhelming:

1. His enemies were there. They had come to watch Him die. They were not about to leave without being satisfied.

2. The soldiers assigned to the execution were there. They had seen many men die because that was their business. They were experts at declaring, "He's gone."

3. Joseph of Arimathea was there. He was a prominent man who did not become rich by letting people pull the wool over his eyes. He provided the tomb and would not have been interested in doing that for a live man.

4. The women were there. They were accustomed to serving at funerals. They knew death when they saw it.

5. Jesus' disciples were there. And because they knew He was dead, they ran and hid. "It's over. When will they be coming for us?" So they went to an upper room behind closed doors. They were like the Jewish people during the time of Hitler—hiding away, not wanting to be discovered, afraid for their lives.

Take Up the Cross and March

Jesus faced the cross intentionally. Without the cross, He would not have been the Messiah. And Jesus challenges us to face the cross. Without the cross, we are not worthy to be His disciples. Jesus said, "If anyone wishes to come after Me, let him deny himself, and take up his cross, and follow Me" (Matthew 16:24).

But what does that mean? Does it mean that we are to be literally nailed to some wood? No, but it does mean that we are to be willing to do at least the following:

1. Allow God's will to take priority over our feelings. In the Garden of Gethsemane, Jesus did not feel like going to the cross. Nevertheless, He said, "Not my will but thine be done."

2. When we know the needs of others, we need to be willing to deny selfishness to meet those needs (1 John 3:16, 17).

3. We are not to retaliate. Jesus could have asked legions of angels to spare Him from having to endure the cross. But He did not. We are all fortunate that it was Jesus on the cross and not I. Knowing what I know today, I might not have called down angels, but I think I would have been prone to call into existence a dozen jet bombers and twenty-five tanks. Those people had never seen an airplane, experienced a bomb, nor seen a tank. I would have done something spectacular, something that the world would never forget. But Jesus did things differently, and the world has never forgotten. Nor has it ever got over it.

4. While we may be hurting personally, we should be sensitive to how others around us are hurting. Jesus was in pain, but He did what He had always done. He considered what others might be going through and ministered to them. He saw His mother and knew her pain; so He asked the disciple whom He loved to take care of His mother.

5. We should not seek to draw attention to ourselves. Jesus could have come down from the cross and made quite an impression. But He chose to die instead.

6. We must forgive those who hurt us. Jesus forgave those who were causing Him so much pain. It is not so difficult to forgive those who offend us or hurt us unintentionally. There are times that the accidental mistakes of others have caused us trouble and made things difficult for us.

Some time ago I read about a man in northern California who was scheduled for surgery to have his right leg amputated. The surgeon misread the order and amputated his left leg instead. When the mistake was discovered, the right leg had to be immediately amputated.

When the man was told about the mistake and that both of his legs were gone, he replied, "Everyone makes mistakes. I have made many. I hold no grudge."

Such a thing would be hard to forgive, but it is even more difficult to forgive those who have done us in on purpose; they planned to do it. They schemed against us, and they were glad they did us in. That was Jesus' situation. He extended forgiveness on the cross, "Father, forgive them; for they do not know what they are doing" (Luke 23:34). They knew they were crucifying a man, but they did not know the implications of it.

When Jesus reached out in forgiveness, He was in a sense saying, "Everyone can make mistakes. Even if you cut off both of My legs, I have something for you—eternal legs, eternal arms, an eternal heart, and eternal salvation—if you are willing to come to the Father through Me."

Living out the cross means making decisions for the benefit of others, even when the cost factor diminishes self.

The Resurrection

Jesus does not challenge us with the sacrifice of the cross without the promise of the resurrection.

Many of us have seen it—a formation of jet planes flying by in honor of a flyer who has been killed. The formation is done with perfect flying, but there is something different about the formation. A space in the formation is left empty; the empty space reminds the viewers that the dead person is no longer among the flyers.

There is another empty space that reminds us of the absence of a person. The empty tomb reminds us that Jesus is no longer among the dead. He arose from the dead and touched the living with significance, meaningfulness, and challenge.

We, too, have experienced a resurrection in this life as we put on Christ through baptism. That is our first resurrection, and those of us who are still alive on earth are living a resurrected life now in the resurrected power of Jesus. We will experience another resurrection after physical death. But our resurrection after our death to sin should be lived out in a way that people can see a newness of life.

Jesus arose to meet people where they were. Are you in a state of disappointment? Women came to the tomb while it was still dark. They did not wait for the full sun; consequently, they could not see clearly. Isn't that the way some of us are? Life is not always bright for us. Some lights have been turned off. Some bulbs have burned out. Some shades have been pulled down. Perhaps we have lost a friend or a job, the bills are piling up, or the child support is not being paid. Everyday with Jesus is not always sweeter than the day before.

Some of our darkness is caused by our grief. It happened then with Mary. (See John 20:11-18.) She was standing outside of the tomb, crying, "I don't know where He is." Aren't we like that? Through the tears of disappointment, desperation, and depression, we may ask, "Where are you, God? Life is caving in. It is unraveling. I don't know where to look for You."

And then Jesus met her where she was. "Mary." Jesus also knows you by name. Mary turned around and saw Jesus. We need to turn around. We need to quit looking just at the negatives, the problems, the disappointments, and the setbacks. It is difficult to see someone with your back to him and your eyes full of tears. Turn around, and He can wipe away your tears. And He will say, "You are not alone. Lo, I am with you always."

As Jesus' resurrected life approached people who were in a state of disappointment, so you and I in our newness of His resurrection could reach out to touch people who are in a doom-and-gloom situation.

Do you have an embarrassing past? That was Mary Magdalene. She had been filled with demons, and some suggest that she may have sold her body to men for a living. If so, would any man really care about her? Then Jesus came to her—risen and alive. He gave her the opportunity to be the first to tell others. A woman who perhaps had torn homes apart was now assigned to the task of bringing hope to people. She came as a spectator and left as a participant with the risen Jesus.

We must reach out to people with embarrassing pasts and let them know that their future can be different because Christ is alive. He is alive in us here and now.

Are you someone who grew up in the church, attending all the sunrise services, Sunday morning, Sunday evening, and midweek services, but you got away from the church and then began to live on your own? We live in a fast-moving society—we drive fast, eat fast, think fast, talk fast, decide fast, and spend fast. Sometimes we get tired of it all—fast. We decide it is not worth all of the hassle. We want to bail out. So we turn our backs on the straight life.

A man may go to the sports car route or get a classic pickup truck or a motorcycle. He may buy a new wardrobe, open his shirt down to his navel, and wear a necklace. He may want a young woman on his arm.

A woman may go to "have her colors done," get a sports car, get a new wardrobe, and start going out with a younger man.

But it is not long before the car wears out, the clothes go out of style, the young companion disappears, and birthdays come and go. The person wakes up, realizing that life without God and the church is empty indeed.

All the disciples had turned their backs on Jesus and run out on Him. They had become A.W.O.L.: deserters, quitters, drop outs, burn outs, and runaways. But then in His resurrected life, Jesus came to them—risen and alive. In a sense, He was saying to them, "I died for you. I know that you quit, but I believe in you. I still care for you. My open arms are wider than your closed hearts. I will not lock you into your rejection of Me. That was yesterday. I want to give you a chance to be Mine."

Peter had denied Jesus three times, and so three times Jesus gave him the chance to say, "I love you, Jesus." (See John 21:15-17.)

As the resurrected Jesus became the reconciling friend to those who turned their backs on Him, we need to journey through life doing the same—reaching out to people who may have given their lives to Christ at one time but later turned their backs on Him. We dare not do less than Jesus. That is part of what it means to live on the Heaven-bound way.

The risen Christ sees the facade, yet He loves the clod that He made out of the sod; how odd! And it is odd, until we turn around and see that the risen Jesus has nail-pierced hands.

There are people today who feel hemmed in and afraid as the disciples did after Jesus' death. People today lock themselves behind locked doors—the door of economy (we borrow more), the door of aging (we cover it up), the door of disease (we will not admit it), the door of broken relationships (we will not risk entering into another one). What they need is what the disciples needed. They need the risen body of Christ, knocking on their doors with a reconciling word, "Peace."

The life of the resurrected Jesus now lives in Christians. We are the dwelling place of God. Christians collectively are called the body of Christ. Let's transport Him in our journey through life.

The people took Jesus down from the cross. They thought they had got Him out of the way forever. They wrapped Him up like a mummy and put one hundred pounds of spices within the wrapping. They put Him in a tomb and closed the entrance with a huge boulder. They put armed guards outside of the tomb. They sealed it with a Roman seal so that if anyone broke it, he would be liable to execution. They did what they could to keep Him out of people's lives forever. "We've got Him. We've killed Him. We've secured His body. He is in that tomb to stay forever. He will never get out."

But that was on Friday. Sunday was coming. And Sunday came! Up from the grave He arose! And He arose for the purpose of being involved in the lives of people—even those who had killed Him, even those who had quit on Him.

Because we are Christians, many in the world will do everything they can to keep us buried—so we don't get involved in social issues or community involvements. But as the Christ in the tomb could not be buried—put out of sight and involvement—the Christ in the heart of the Christian cannot be buried—detached, disconnected, uninvolved in the lives of people.

And now He calls us to be His ongoing resurrected body, reaching out, caring, loving, reconciling, forgiving, touching the lives of people with the attitude, the grace, and the love of Jesus. That's Heaven-bound living.

As the resurrected life of Jesus then was power, so the resurrected life of Jesus in us today is power in us that can make a difference.

No wonder the apostle Paul said that he counted everything else as insignificant compared to knowing Christ "and the power of His resurrection" (Philippians 3:7-10). The Greek word for power is the word from which we get our word *dynamite*.

The dynamite of Jesus' resurrection in us is the Holy Spirit. And the fruit of that dynamite is manifold. When we want to get even, it is dynamite to forgive. When we want to blow our tops, it is dynamite to be patient. When we want to be unfaithful to our mates, to our kids, to our employers, to our employees, to our friends, to ourselves, and to God, it is dynamite to be trustworthy. When we want to blame others, it's dynamite to accept responsibility ourselves. When we want to bury our heads, it is dynamite to lift them high. When we want to run away from sacrifice and service, it is dynamite to stay. When we want to stay in sinful situations, it is a dynamite to flee from them. When we want to retaliate, it is dynamite to leave the vengeance to God.

The psychologist William James once said that the greatest use of life is to spend it for something that will outlast it. Jesus outlasted life, and so will we—if we become a participant and not spectator in the cross and resurrection of Jesus.

It is not enough for the world to read about it two thousand years ago. The world must see it today in you and me.

You may have seen the famous symbol of an ox quietly standing between an altar and plow on a plaque somewhere. It expresses the attitude that fits our Heaven-bound journey. Underneath the symbol are words, "Ready for either or for both." We are ready to serve (with the plow) or to be a sacrifice (on the altar).

CHAPTER ELEVEN

GROW OR DIE

Matthew 28:16-20

A modern parable gets at the heart of the Christian mission and, at the same time, gets at the heart of part of our problem.

On a dangerous seacoast where shipwrecks often occur, there was once a little life-saving station. The building was primitive, and there was just one boat, but the members of the life-saving station were committed and kept a constant watch over the sea. When a ship went down, they unselfishly went out day or night to save the lost. Because so many lives were saved by that station, it became famous.

Consequently, many people wanted to be associated with the station to give their time, talent, and money to support its important work. New boats were bought, new crews were recruited, a formal training session was offered.

As the membership in the life-saving station grew, some of the members became unhappy that the building was so primitive and that the equipment was so outdated. They wanted a better place to welcome the survivors pulled from the sea. So they replaced the emergency cots with beds and put better furniture in the enlarged and newly decorated building.

Now the life-saving station became a popular gathering place for its members. They met regularly; and when they did, it was apparent how they loved one another. They greeted each other, hugged each other, and shared with one another the events that had been going on in their lives. But fewer members were now interested in going to sea on life-saving missions; so they hired lifeboat crews to do this for them.

About this time, a large ship was wrecked off of the coast, and the hired crews brought into the life-saving station boatloads of cold, wet, dirty, sick, and half-drowned people. Some of them had black skin, and some had yellow skin. Some could speak English well, and some could hardly speak it at all. Some were first-class cabin passengers of the ship, and some were the deck hands.

The beautiful meeting place became a place of chaos. The plush carpets got dirty. Some of the exquisite furniture got scratched. So the property committee immediately had a shower built outside the house where the victims of shipwreck could be cleaned up before coming inside.

At the next meeting, there was rift in the membership. Most of the members wanted to stop the club's life-saving activities, for they were unpleasant and a hindrance to the normal fellowship of the members. Other members insisted that life-saving was their primary purpose and pointed out that they were still called a life-saving station. But they were finally voted down and told that if they wanted to save the lives of all those various kinds of people who would be shipwrecked, they could begin their own life-saving station down the coast. And do you know what? That is what they did.

As the years passed, the new station experienced the same changes that had occurred in the old. It evolved into a place to meet regularly for fellowship, for committee meetings, and for special training sessions about their mission, but few went out to the drowning people. The drowning people were no longer welcomed in that new life-saving station. So another life-saving station was founded further down the coast. History continued to repeat itself. And if you visit that seacoast today, you will find a number of adequate meeting places with ample parking and plush carpeting. Shipwrecks are frequent in those waters, *but most of the people drown.*[2]

God is getting tired of hearing, "But most of the people drown." And wouldn't you—if those people were members of your family, or people you knew and loved?

A man named Bill was walking not far from the beach one morning when he heard something. Someone was yelling. Then it came again, and Bill realized that it was a desperate call for help. He started running toward the beach. When he got there, he saw that a lad was going under the water. It was apparent that he was not going to make it back up. So Bill dived into the water, swam to the boy, found him, and brought him to the surface. When they got to the shore, the lad was not breathing. Bill provided mouth-to-mouth resuscitation until he began to breathe again.

Which part of Bill's body was the most important in saving that boy's life? Or to ask it another way, which part of Bill's body was not needed? Was it the ears that heard the cry? How about the mind that interpreted the cry for help? How about the legs that ran to the scene? Or the glands that pumped more energy into Bill? Or the arms and legs that gave momentum to the swim? Or was it his mouth that helped the boy breathe again?

Certainly, the answer is obvious. Every part of Bill's body was important in saving that boy.

The church is called the body of Christ. Which part of that body is most important? Or, to say it another way, which part is not necessary in saving the spiritually drowning people of this world? Is saving the lost the role of the preacher only? How about the Sunday-school teachers? How about the paid staff members? How about the custodian? What about those who come and sit in the pew as "full members" of this "life-saving station"? The answer is obvious. God has called every part of His body to be involved in reconciling people to Him.

---

[2] My paraphrase of the original parable by Thomas Wedel, *Ecumenical Review,* October, 1953.

We cannot dodge His great commission to us, which is stated in various different ways in the Scriptures:

> And Jesus came up and spoke to them, saying, "All authority has been given to Me in heaven and on earth.
> "Go therefore and make disciples of all the nations, baptizing them in the name of the Father and the Son and the Holy Spirit, teaching them to observe all that I commanded you; and lo, I am with you always, even to the end of the age" (Matthew 28:18-20).

> And He said to them, "Go into all the world and preach the gospel to all creation.
> "He who has believed and has been baptized shall be saved; but he who has disbelieved shall be condemned" (Mark 16:15, 16).

> And He said to them, "Thus it is written, that the Christ should suffer and rise again from the dead the third day; and that repentance for forgiveness of sins should be proclaimed in His name to all the nations, beginning from Jerusalem" (Luke 24:46, 47).

> But you shall receive power when the Holy Spirit has come upon you; and you shall be My witnesses both in Jerusalem, and in all Judea and Samaria, and even to the remotest part of the earth (Acts 1:8).

> Now all these things are from God, who reconciled us to Himself through Christ, and gave us the ministry of reconciliation, namely, that God was in Christ reconciling the world to Himself, not counting their trespasses against them, and He has committed to us the word of reconciliation.
> Therefore, we are ambassadors for Christ, as though God were entreating through us; we beg you on behalf of Christ, be reconciled to God (2 Corinthians 5:18-20).

A commission is really a call for us to be in a co-mission with God to journey with Him. Is our response anywhere close to Paul's? He declared, "I am under obligation both to the Greeks and to barbarians, both to the wise and to the foolish. Thus, for my part, I am eager to preach the gospel to you also who are in Rome. For I am not ashamed of the gospel, for it is the power of God for salvation to everyone who believes, to the Jew first and also to the Greek" (Romans 1:14-16).

There were more Christians on the earth percentage-wise at the end of the first century than there are today. How well are we doing? If we continue reconciling people to God through Christ at the pace we have been, and if the population of the world continues to rise at the present rate, by the end of this century only fifteen per cent of the world's population will have any connection to Christ. How well are we doing?

There are presently over 17,000 unreached people groups. Now I don't mean 17,000 people, but people-*groups!* There are presently 5000 different languages that have not yet been penetrated with the Christian message. How well are we doing?

There is not one cross-cultural Christian representative and thus not one church in any one of the 17,000 people groups that have not been reached for Christ. How's our journey?

If those who have had absolutely no contact with the Christian message were lined up five-deep, and we got in a car and drove past the line at fifty miles per hour—twenty-four hours a day—it would take us three and a half years to get to the end of the line. And by the time we got there, the line would be 26,000 miles longer. How's our journey?

That God's commission is for us today is seen in many different ways in Scripture, especially in the call of God, the intention of Jesus, and the condition of man.

God's Journey

God's journey for His people has always included two dimensions. Those two dimensions are like a two-sided coin. It takes both sides to make a legitimate, spendable coin. If a coin comes out of the mint with only one side printed, it is worthless. The two dimensions of God's journey could be labeled in many different ways:

One	Two
Journey to forgiveness	Journey to function
Journey with gifts	Journey with demands
Journey with rootage	Journey with fruitage
Journey with privilege	Journey with purpose

The first dimension includes what God provides for us on this journey. His forgiveness, His gifts, and privileges. That is God's initiative, God's doing, God's provisions. The second involves our response to God's provisions. God wants to send us on our journey with privileges (what He provides) and purpose (what He expects from us).

This two-dimensional journey goes as far back as the journey Abraham took. Look at it in Genesis 12:2, 3:

> I will make you a great nation [privilege], and I will bless you [privilege], and I will make your name great [privilege], and so you will be a blessing [purpose]; and I will bless those who bless you [privilege], and the one who curses you I will curse [privilege]. And in you all the families of the earth shall be blessed [purpose].

God's journey was begun through one man, Abraham, and from that one man to the entire nation. But as the population of the nation grew, the people began to emphasize the privilege side and de-emphasize the purpose side. "We are privileged—we have the right God, the right rituals, the right ordinances, the right day of worship, and the right book." But the more they emphasized their privileges (inward orientation), the less they emphasized their purpose (outward orientation).

By the time the prophets spoke, the privilege and purpose sides had become so out of balance that the primary message of the prophets was this, "Repent and get the privilege and purpose back into balance." Let's look at one example (out of hundreds) to illustrate. Isaiah 5 begins by affirming a love relationship:

"Let me sing now for my well-beloved a song of my beloved concerning His vineyard. My well-beloved had a vineyard on a fertile hill" (Isaiah 5:1). Notice the privilege and purpose aspects that appear in verse 2:

And He dug it all around, removed its stones, and planted it with the choicest vine. And He built a tower in the middle of it, and hewed out a wine vat in it [privileges], *then He expected it to produce good grapes* [purpose], but it produced only worthless ones [out of balance].

Then God asked a penetrating question, "And now, O inhabitants of Jerusalem and men of Judah, judge between Me and My vineyard. What more was there to do for My vineyard that I have not done in it?" (Isaiah 5:3, 4)

God was willing to take the blame for the vineyard's not producing good grapes *if* He had withheld an essential privilege from the vineyard. Did He? Of course, the answer is no. Why, then, did it not produce good grapes?

What was God talking about? He was talking about His people, who were not producing, "For the vineyard of the Lord of hosts is the house of Israel, and the men of Judah His delightful plant" (Isaiah 5:7).

God's people continued to keep privilege and purpose out of balance. But then one person came to earth who had the perfect balance between the two aspects. That one was Jesus. He was privileged with God's Holy Spirit, and He lived out the purpose of being God's reconciling Messiah for the hurting and lost mankind all around Him.

Grab ahold of this privilege-purpose concept, and the Bible will become clearer to you. Some entire New Testament books are organized around these two aspects. The first eleven chapters of Romans primarily tells us what God has done for us (privilege); then chapters 12 through 16 unfold our purpose. The first three chapters of Ephesians emphasizes God's privileges, while the last three outline the dimensions of God's purpose.

It is difficult to get through many pages in the New Testament without seeing privilege and purpose. One of the finest summaries is found in 2 Corinthians 5:17-20:

Therefore if any man is in Christ, he is a new creature; the old things passed away; behold, new things have come [privilege].

Now all these things are from God [privilege] who reconciled us to Himself through Christ [privilege], and gave us the ministry of reconciliation [purpose], namely, that God was in Christ reconciling the world to Himself [privilege] not, counting their trespasses against them [privilege], and He has committed to us the word of reconciliation [purpose].

Therefore, we are ambassadors for Christ, as though God were entreating through us; we beg you on behalf of Christ, be reconciled to God [purpose].

"But most of the people drown." Isn't God getting tired of that?

Jesus' Intentional Journey

From before Jesus was born, His intention was announced, "And she will bear a Son; and you shall call His name Jesus, for it is He who will save His people from their sins" (Matthew 1:21). John the Baptist declared it: "Behold, the Lamb of God who takes away the sin of the world" (John 1:29).

Jesus himself declared it: "For the Son of Man has come to seek and to save that which was lost" (Luke 19:10). Jesus' death declared it: "He Himself bore our sins in His body on the cross, that we might die to sin and live to righteousness; for by His wounds you were healed" (1 Peter 2:24).

Jesus' resurrection certifies it: He was "raised because of our justification" (Romans 4:25). Jesus' commission calls us to participate in it, "Go therefore and make disciples of all the nations, baptizing them in the name of the Father and the Son and the Holy Spirit" (Matthew 28:19).

Our linkage with Jesus demands that we participate in reconciling others to God through Him. Is it possible that the purpose is weakened because we may not really believe that a person in sin is lost eternally?

Those We Pass By

From the very beginning, God was clear. Sin will bring spiritual death—the separation of man from God. When man dies physically and his spirit is separated from God, he lives forever in total exclusion from God's presence— that is Hell.

What causes that? "The wages of sin is death" (Romans 6:23). Wages are what we earn, what we deserve. We have a right to our wages. If I would offer you $50 to do a job for me, and I gave you $50 when you did it—then I would be just. What if, after you did the job, I decided to give you only $10? Then I would be unjust. Or what if after I gave you the $50, I then said, "I know your wages are $50, but I would like to make a trade with you. Give me back your wages, and I will give you $25,000." Would that be just? No, it would not be just; it would be gracious.

That is the way God is with us. Although we have earned the wags of sin (death), His grace offers us the gift of eternal life in Jesus Christ. "By grace you have been saved through faith" (Ephesians 2:8).

Human history can be wrapped up in one verse, "For the wages of sin is death, but the free gift of God is eternal life in Christ Jesus our Lord" (Romans 6:23).

Jesus is Heaven's immortal medicine (life) for the terminal condition (death) that is caused by sin. It makes no difference whether a person understands it or not, sin brings the terminal condition.

It has a parallel in the physical world. It does not make any difference whether or not we understand about a disease. If a disease hits us and has a terminal nature, we are in a terminal nature regardless of our understanding about it.

Some people have said, "If people in other countries have never heard of God or Jesus, then they will be saved because a just God would not let them go to Hell." That position violates the entire teaching of the Bible. There are people all over the world who have never heard of medicines that we have in the United States. If they had some of them, their diseases could be cured or helped. But having them on our shelves is not helping those people. The medicine has to come into contact with them. A cure on our shelves here does not help the condition of people elsewhere unless that cure can get to them.

So it is in the spiritual realm. Christ is of no value to the lost unless and until we connect Christ up with the lost. If people are saved because they have never heard, then the best thing we could do would be to be sure that nobody lets the truth out. The greatest thing we could do for the salvation of mankind would be to shoot a person as soon as he received Christ so that person could go immediately to Heaven and not tell someone who had never heard. The best thing God could have done would have been to have had Jesus die on an isolated island so no one would know anything about it. Then when we die, He could say to us, "Surprise! Christ died for you. But because you didn't know anything about it, your sins are forgiven and you are saved."

That violates the totality of Biblical truth. Jesus came in flesh and for everyone to see. Jesus commanded that we go and tell others. Jesus declared, "I am the way, and the truth, and the life; no one comes to the Father, but through me" (John 14:6). When Jesus said, "No one," He made no exceptions—whether one has heard or not.

It is as inappropriate to keep Christ away from people who have been bitten by the virus of sin as it would have been to keep the polio vaccine away from people who needed that.

The Opportunities Along the Way

The message in the book of Acts is that the gospel is for all kinds of people—no one is excluded. It is for the Jews, the rich, the poor, the healthy, the sick, the young, the old, men, women, philosophers, and everyone else. Acts also demonstrates that Christians are to seize any and every opportunity to share Christ with others. The first evangelistic endeavor happened at the "sacred" place of the temple. But it got out of the temple and into the streets. It could happen at unplanned times, such as on the way to the "sacred" meeting. It could happen in the process of doing benevolent work. It could happen in a hitchhiking situation. For the apostle Paul, it could happen in prison, at a women's prayer meeting, at a church conference, when encountering a sick situation, while traveling on a ship, while visiting in a household, in a planned preaching setting, in a meeting with city officials, or at a gathering of community philosophers.

Paul utilized both the positive and negative opportunities to share Christ. He evidently had to make changes in his travel plans due to sickness and so preached to the Galatians because of that change (Galatians 4:13-15). Because of his appeal to Caesar and his transferal to Rome for trial, he was able to evangelize the imperial guard and even some in Caesar's own household (Philippians 1:1; 4:22). During his imprisonment at Philippi, he was able to evangelize the jailer (Acts 16). While in his Roman imprisonment, he evangelized a runaway slave, Onesimus, and sent him back to his owner as more than a slave—as a reconciled brother (Philemon).

While in prison, Paul took time to pray, to meditate, to reflect, and to write several letters that motivated the church then and still today (Ephesians, Colossians, Philippians, Philemon, and 2 Timothy).

I will never forget it. It happened in the late 1950s at an Air Force Base in Japan. I was the supervisor of the control tower there.

A pilot called in with a distressed voice, "I just lost my wing man." The controllers knew what that meant and picked up the red crash phone immediately. When that phone was picked up, rescue helicopters were to be in the air within minutes. The controllers gave permission to the pilot to descend below the clouds and see if he could locate his downed partner. And he did. The other pilot had ejected out of the jet fighter and was spotted in the sea.

In the next few moments, the lead pilot spoke words that remain unforgettable.

"I've spotted him. He's in the water."

Seconds later: "He does not have his life raft inflated. He seems to be tangled up in the parachute chord. Where's the rescue team?"

Seconds later: "He is still tangled up in the chord and on the water without a raft. Where's the rescue team?"

Seconds later: "He's getting tired. I'm not sure how much longer he can stay on top of the water. Where's the rescue team?"

Seconds later: "He is going under. No, he is back up now. Where is that rescue team?"

Later: "He's going under again. He's not coming up this time. Where's that rescue team?"

Later: "I can still see him, but he is still under the water. He's sinking deeper. We've lost him. He's gone. Where is that rescue team?"

This happened at the Christmas season, when traffic and activities were lighter than usual on the base. In the investigation that followed, it was discovered that the helicopter rescue team—thinking that they would not be needed because of the lax time—decided to fly to a nearby Navy base, which had the biggest shopping facility in the entire area. The team was leisurely Christmas shopping when the question rang out over the airways, "Where is the rescue team?"

Twenty-five years later, I shared this story with an audience in the Midwest. A man came up to me at the end of the service and said, "It is indeed a small, small world. I was one of the pilots flying in the area and had gone to the location to circle the search area. I remember the event well, and that pilot's comments still burn in my heart— 'Where is that rescue team?'"

This world is filled with people who have "bailed out" and are floating and losing their grip. Others have their life rafts inflated, but those rafts are only temporary. Some have holes in them. All are insufficient. And in various ways, the people are asking the question, "Where is the rescue team?"

The Rescuer is Jesus. He is the guide on our journey through life. He says, "Truly, truly, I say to you, he who hears My word, and believes Him who sent Me, has eternal life, and does not come into judgment, but has passed out of death into life" (John 5:24).

But where is the rescue team? What are the rescue activities? Where are those who are traveling on the Heaven-bound road, and what are they doing?

The question is still ringing in the air, "Where is the rescue team?"

May we answer, "We are here. We are eager. And we are coming!"

CHAPTER TWELVE

GOD WILL TURN YOUR FROWNS INTO CROWNS

Revelation 21:1-8

God has promised it, "Blessed is a man who perseveres under trial; for once he has been approved, he will receive the crown of life, which the Lord has promised to those who love Him" (James 1:12). Trials are problems, setbacks, disappointments, and frustrations. With trials come frowns, but God will turn our frowns into crowns.

The One who is the same yesterday, today, and forever—the One who is the first and last—the One who was dead and has come to life said, "Be faithful until death, and I will give you the crown of life" (Revelation 2:10). That's because Jesus is not only on the journey with us, but He has gone on ahead of us and is getting our tomorrows ready.

When Jesus said that He was going to prepare a place for us (John 14:3), the first place He went was to the cross, then to the tomb; then He arose from the tomb. As a result, our hearts could be cleansed and forgiven. Then His Spirit could come and reside within us.

What a promise! What a provision! What a presence! Are you troubled that Jesus is no longer walking on earth? Are you troubled that you cannot see or hear Him as did those in the first century? Do not fret! Jesus fulfilled His promise, "I will come to you; I will be in you; I will abide in you." He is not just there, but also here.

Sure, life has its down times, its disappointments, its heartaches. But remember, we are not earth-bound but Heaven-bound—and God will turn you frowns into crowns.

The promise was first fulfilled by the sending of the Holy Spirit, who is the extended earthly presence of Jesus himself.

Heaven-bound

If Jesus' promise was only for the here and now, we might sing the song, "Is that all there is?" But Jesus in the here and now is not all there is. He is the Eternal One. He is the Immortal One. His promise to prepare a dwelling place extends beyond earth to Heaven. God's permanent dwelling place is in Heaven, and there is plenty of room for everyone.

When He said, "I go to prepare a place for you," He did not only mean the cross and the tomb (to get our hearts ready for the presence of His Spirit), but He also meant an actual place in Heaven. He ascended into Heaven and is at the right hand of the Father, interceding for us. And He is coming back. Those who have allowed Him to reside in their hearts will be allowed to reside in a place in Heaven with Him.

Heaven is a prepared place for a prepared people. In Heaven, God will eternally dwell among His people (Revelation 21:3).

What will Heaven be like? Any description of Heaven in human words will fall far short of the reality. We can only scratch the surface of the beauty, magnificence, and extravagance of Heaven.

Heaven will be like *a perfect marriage feast:* "And I saw the holy city, new Jerusalem, coming down out of heaven from God, made ready as a bride adorned for her husband" (Revelation 21:2). This verse paints the picture of a ceremonial celebration of the union of Christ and His bride, the church. It will be the beginning of a wedding banquet, like no wedding ever seen on earth (Matthew 22:1-14; Revelation 19:5-9).

Heaven will be *a face-to-face relationship* with God. The dwelling of God is with men, and He will live with them. They will be His people, and God himself will be their God (Revelation 21:3; 22:5).

Heaven will be *the perfect experience.* Nothing will be against us; everything will be for us. The consequences of

112

sin (ours or another's), the violations of earth's laws (such as the law of gravity), and the mortal nature of our physical existence cause our heartbreaks, disappointments, disease, and pain on earth. Those things will not be in Heaven.

In Heaven, perfect love will reign. When perfect love controls everyone's existence, all problems will cease. The perishable will become imperishable, the mortal will become immortal, the temporary will become permanent, and nothing will threaten that. In Heaven there will be no grief, no death, no tears, no crying, and no pain. All of those things will pass away. God will make all things new (Revelation 21:4, 5).

Heaven will provide *eternal security*. That is symbolized by the description of the great high walls and gates. Walls and gates were for security purposes. Although we will have nothing that can invade us or cause us to be insecure, the eternal security is pictured for us in this way. The devil cannot penetrate with his schemes and deceptions (Revelation 21:12, 13).

Heaven will have *the perfect crowd*. All of God's people will be there, including the twelve tribes of Israel and the twelve apostles (Revelation 21:12-14). Anyone who is in Christ will be in Heaven, for it is in Christ that we have received redemption, forgiveness, holiness, and blamelessness (Ephesians 1:3-7).

In Heaven, we will discover how foolish we were to enter into denominational quarrels over various interpretations and hobby horses. In Christ, all human barriers are broken down (Ephesians 2). Those in Christ make up one body and one family, even though they may not recognize it now. No denomination or fellowship on earth has a corner on being God's only people. The sooner we can understand that, the better we can get on with living a life of unity here on earth. We will have to put up with one another forever. Shouldn't we start to practice it now? Why do we have to fuss and fight and fail to recognize that others are our brothers and sisters even though they may meet in different family circles?

Heaven will have *perfect beauty*. It is described in the most magnificent human terms (Revelation 21:15-21)— great and flawless will be the beauty that will saturate

Heaven. We will not have to go a long way to see beauty. It will be around us constantly.

Heaven will have the *perfect access*. The temple with its restrictions will not be there because we will not need any temporary access to God. "For because the Lord God, the Almighty, and the Lamb are its temple" (Revelation 21:22). We will all have immediate and personal access to God. What an opportunity! There will be no upmanship, no competition.

Heaven will have *perfect illumination*. The sun and the moon will not be there to dispel darkness, for the glory of God gives the light (Revelation 21:23; 22:5). Heaven will be filled with *perfect actions and reactions in relationships*. There will be no hint of rebellion there. "The nations shall walk by its light, and the kings of the earth shall bring their glory into it" (Revelation 21:24). No one will try to usurp the authority of God nor put down his peers. No one will have to lock his doors at night in order to sleep soundly (Revelation 21:25, 26).

Heaven will have a *perfect ecology*. Nothing impure will be in the air, water, or food. "Nothing impure will ever enter it, nor will anyone who does what is shameful or deceitful, but only those whose names are written in the Lamb's book of life" (Revelation 21:27, NIV). Heaven will have the *perfect resources* that will result in perfect health. The water of life is as clear as crystal, and the fruit and leaves of the tree of life keep health and prevent any curse from being named or known (Revelation 22:1-3).

Heaven will be a *perfect blessing*. "'Behold, I am coming quickly, and My reward is with Me, to render to every man according to what he has done. I am the Alpha and the Omega, the first and the last, the beginning and the end.' Blessed are those who wash their robes, that they may have the right to the tree of life, and may enter by the gates into the city" (Revelation 22:12-14).

Heaven is for people who journey through life in Christ.

Certain categories of people will not be there, including the unbelieving ones (the atheists), the abominable, murderers, immoral persons (sexual perverts), sorcerers, drug addicts, and idolaters. These people are guilty of *big sins!* But there is one that heads the list and another that ends the list that may not seem as big to us: "the cowardly" heads the list; "the liars" ends the list.

It might be possible that one reason we fail to bear fruit is because we are cowards. We don't want the flak that might come to us if we bear testimony about Christ and allow His nature to live in us when His nature may not be a part of those around us. To be cowardly is also to be a liar, for it camouflages and detours the truth, and deceives the people around us.

Listen to what Paul says:

> Do you not know that the unrighteous shall not inherit the kingdom of God? Do not be deceived; neither fornicators, nor idolaters, nor adulterers, nor effeminate, nor homosexuals, nor thieves, not the covetous, nor drunkards, nor revilers, nor swindlers, shall inherit the kingdom of God (1 Corinthians 6:9, 10).

Paul's teaching agrees with what we read in the book of Revelation—"their part will be in the lake that burns with fire and brimstone, which is the second death" (Revelation 21:8); this is what happens to the unrighteous.

But wait a minute! Paul also added, "And such were some of you; but you were washed, but you were sanctified, but you were justified in the name of the Lord Jesus Christ, and in the Spirit of God" (1 Corinthians 6:11). God turns frowns into crowns!

The church in the first century was filled with people with sordid backgrounds who had turned away from their past and had turned toward God through Jesus Christ. In that turn, they were forgiven. They were cleansed. They were adopted. They were born again. They became dwelling places of God. He turned their frowns into crowns.

None of those in the church then would have made that change had others not been journeying toward Heaven and invited them to go along. Christian living here is Heaven-bound living, but not in neglect of the hurts around us here on earth.

If we want to be in God's presence in Heaven, we need to allow Him to dwell within us and empower us now. If we want to live in the perfect world, we need to be influencing our world now. If we want access to God in Heaven, we need to give Him access to our lives now. If we want perfect illumination in Heaven, we need to walk in the light of His Word now. If we want to live in purity then, we must become more pure now. If we want to participate in the perfect blessing then, we need to live as God's blessings now.

In short, if we want to live in Heaven, we must first accept His invitation now. "The Spirit and the bride say, 'Come.' And let him who hears say, 'Come.' And let the one who is thirsty come; let the one who wishes take the water of life without cost" (Revelation 22:17).

But accepting the invitation is not enough. Since we live by the Spirit, let us keep in step with the Spirit (Galatians 5:25). If we say we are Christians, we ought to walk in the same manner as He walked (1 John 2:6).

Conclusion

We are born physically to grow and we are born spiritually to grow. Being born again is the beginning. Maturity is the continuation. Our journey is the bridge we cross from infancy to maturity.

But we don't walk that bridge alone. He walks with us, in us, and through us. It is not by our strength and intelligence; it is by His Spirit.

The song says it, "Walkin' on the Heaven road; I'm gonna lay down my heavy load, 'Cause Jesus said He'd walk along with me.... So why not come along and join me on the Heaven road?"

He will turn your frowns and crowns.

CHAPTER THIRTEEN

WATCH OUT FOR SNARES AND TRAPS

James 1:14-16

The Heaven-bound journey is an unselfish journey as we look out for the needs of others along the way and reach out to touch them as Jesus did. But it is possible to be so sensitive to the needs of others that we neglect ourselves. Paul knew that danger; so he said, "But I buffet my body and make it my slave, lest possibly, after I have preached to others, I myself should be disqualified" (1 Corinthians 9:27).

Paul was an apostle, inspired, directly taught by Jesus, one who had special visions, one who did miracles—and yet he said that he needed to toughen up his body so that he would be a master of his physical desires. If an apostle had that need, will we have it any less?

Jesus understood that we can fall when He told His men to keep watching and praying that they might not enter into temptation, "for the spirit is willing but the flesh is weak." If the flesh was weak for them, isn't it also for us? Paul said to the elders at Ephesus, "Be on guard for yourselves and for all the flock" (Acts 20:28).

Heaven-bound living includes personal holiness. But there is a threat to personal holiness, even for those who stay on the narrow road. It is a threat that is real to all of us. Its name? Temptation. It is a universal threat. It was a threat to Jesus himself. We are told that He was tempted in all points as are we (Hebrews 4:15).

Now Jesus' half brother, James, who grew up with Jesus and then was inspired by Jesus, tells us how temptation worked on Jesus and how it works on us as we journey Heaven-bound. James says that each of us is tempted when we are carried away and enticed by our own desires (James 1:14). Some translations have the word *lust*. But it is the Greek word for any kind of desires that is used here.

Just because we are on the narrow road does not mean we have checked in all of our human desires. They are still with us. The basic desires like hunger, thirst, security, fellowship, and sex are a natural part of our lives. They are all God-given desires. We are Godufactured people.

But God did more than just give us desires that relate to this physical world. He also created a wonderful world in which those desires could be met. For instance, He provided food to meet the desire of hunger; liquid to meet the desire of thirst; himself and others to meet the desire for security and fellowship; male and female to meet the desire for sex.

But God went one step further—He set up guardrails and signposts along our way so that we would not get off the narrow road and crash into disaster. As long as we stay within the guardrails, we have fulfillment. If we get beyond the guardrail, it is like taking a step off a cliff with treacherous rocks below.

Some people like to live on the other side of the guardrail and have not noticed yet how devastating that is. It's like a man who jumped off of a twenty-story building, and as he came by the tenth floor someone yelled out and asked him how he was. He replied as he continued spiraling downward, "So far, everything is just fine."

Around the hunger desire, God put up the guardrail of no gluttony; around the thirst desire, God up the guardrail of no drunkenness; around the sexual desire, God put of the guardrail of marriage. Those are God-given desires with God-given resources and God-given guardrails. But we are tempted by our own desires. I have never been tempted with anything I did not desire. Here is how temptation works. The devil tempts us to go just a bit beyond God's guardrail, and he does it in deceptive ways.

We are tempted when we are "carried away" by our own desires. *Carried away* is from a word that was used by fisherman in the first century. A good translation would be "lured," and some translations read that way. A fisherman lures a fish by baiting a hook; he makes the bait look good and authentic. But what the fish does not see is the hook inside the bait. Can anything be wrong when it looks so good? The devil does that—he makes temptations look authentic, so real, so fulfilling, so glamorous, so "okay." But it is just a bit beyond the guardrail. I have gone after that kind of bait, and so have you.

We are also tempted when we are "enticed" by our own desires. That word was used by hunters. It describes a duck call that hunters would use to get the attention of ducks flying by. The ducks would hear the call and think their friends or relatives were down in the water. They would fly down to join them—but only the hunters were waiting. But it sounded so authentic, so real, so inviting, so safe. That's the way the devil works. He will make it sound so easy, so satisfying, so needed, so safe—but it is beyond the guardrail and contains hidden dangers.

It is so easy for us to forget that devil is alive. He is alive and sick. He has a terminal disease and wants to give it to each of us. He is deceptive. He will do anything to hide the truth; he will use anybody; he will say anything to get us to go beyond the guardrail.

Tony Campollo tells about the time that he and some others entered a dime store at Halloween time and switched the price tags on some items. The devil does that with us. He switches the price tags and causes us to think that things that are valuable are worth only ten cents, and things that have no value are what we should want to possess.

We need to recognize temptations when they come. We need to recognize that the devil is trying to lure us like fish and call to us like ducks. We need to declare to the devil; "I am not a fish and I am not a duck. I am a person made in the image of God. I am on a Heaven-bound journey, and I know that you are trying to detour me from Heaven-bound living. Devil, get out of my life. I am done with you. I am running from you. I love the Lord. I hate you."

God has promised us that none of us will be tempted above what we are able in our present spiritual maturity. God has promised that He is faithful to provide us a way out of every temptation that lures us to get off of the roadway (1 Corinthians 10:13).

There are some escape routes when temptations comes. They are not foolproof. If they were, Christians would never sin. The devil is very deceptive and creative. He understands how we function. When we think we have a foolproof escape route, he knows how to design another way to lure us. That's why each of us must always take heed lest we fall.

Here are some of those escape routes:

Draw Near to God. What do you do when you are in a room that has only a fireplace in it for heat when it starts to get cold? One thing you do is get closer to the fire. In the same way, we are to get close to God. James 4:8 says: "Draw near to God and He will draw near to you." The devil does not like the nearness of God.

We are not only to get close to God, but also be in Him—so much so that we allow Him to be in us. It is one thing to put iron in a fire; but it is something else to keep the iron in the fire long enough so that not only is the iron in the fire, but the fire is also in the iron.

Be committed; don't just feel. Commitment is the only way to stick with something over the long haul. In the Garden of Gethsemane, Jesus made His decision out of commitment—not feeling. Feeling can be so deceptive.

Pete Maravitch, world record-breaking Christian basketball player, did not have the slightest idea that he had a defective heart. He was playing basketball with James Dobson. After the game, Dr. Dobson asked him how he was feeling. He replied, "I have never felt better." A few minutes later, he was dead.

I can understand that. Just seconds before my heart attack, I felt great. As feeling does not always measure our physical health, so feeling does not always measure our spiritual health. It is commitment. Stay on the Heaven-bound road with commitment.

Start despising evil. Paul writes that we are to love what is good and hate what is evil (Romans 12:9). What are you hating these days?

Flee temptation—as if we were trying to get out of a burning building (1 Corinthians 6:18).

120

Refuse the devil. Just say "no."

Resist the devil—as if he were snatching the purse out of your hand (James 4:7). The devil hates resisters. He is a coward; he cannot handle people who stand up to him with courage and strength. That is why cowardice is listed as a sin; it is of the devil (Revelation 21:8).

Toughen Up (1 Corinthians 9:27). Get your physical desires under control. Don't allow them to master you. We need to say from time to time, "Down, baby. I will not let my desires run wild. My body will be my slave. I will not be its slave."

Meditate and draw upon the presence and the power of God (Psalm 119:97).

Ask Jesus to intercede for you. He lives in Heaven to intercede for us so we can continue to be on the Heaven-bound journey with Heaven-bound living (Hebrews 7:25; 9:24; Romans 8:34).

Ask others to intercede. When we sense that we are getting too vulnerable and may be close to being lured or enticed, we need to place ourselves in some kind of accountability to others (1 Samuel 12:23).

Become the master of your senses. We need to understand that "garbage in" eventually leads to "garbage out."

Confess your sins to God. Our confessing invites His cleansing (1 John 1:9).

Remember that God is depending on us. It does make a difference to God's effectiveness because God has chosen to work through His vessels. We are fragile, vulnerable, and breakable vessels.

Trust Jesus. Don't just trust that He is in Heaven, but also trust that He is on the journey with us down here and piloting the airline. He is inside of us. His way is the powerful, pertinent, personal, perceptive, and productive way.

Get scared to death of Hell. We stay away from the things we fear. If we are not afraid of it, we will venture closer to it. If you are not scared of Hell, then get scared. To be scared of Hell does not mean you don't love God. I was scared of being spanked, but I still loved my mother. But being scared of Hell will mean that you do love God and you know that God will not be anywhere near Hell. To be scared of Hell does not mean you are immature. It can, however, mean that you are very mature, for Jesus believed in Hell and taught us to fear it (Matthew 10:28).

We are tempted when we are lured (like fish) with bait and enticed (like birds) with a bird call. So be on the alert. Be on guard. Take your stand and declare to the devil, "Buzz off. Get out of here, Buster. I am not a fish for your bait, and I am not a bird in the sky for your cheap, fake mating calls. I am a person made in the image of God, who is going to send you straight to Hell."

One more bit of good news to remember. We have all sinned and come short of the character of God after we have started down the narrow road. Some of us have sinned in ways we never dreamed we would sin. That doesn't mean the journey is over for us. But it does mean it is time for us to repent because we have hurt God and others. It is time to decide that we want to grow up more and become like Christ. It is not time to rationalize what we did in order to smooth over our wrong, but it is time to be receptive of what God can do with His grace—with His forgiveness, with His love, with His presence with us on this journey.

He is ready with forgiveness. So grace and peace be multiplied to you on this your Heaven-bound journey with Heaven-bound living—Christ in you and you in Christ.

Fasten your seat belts—let's fly!

I Equipment

Water —

Light — Light Unto Our Pathway

II Obstacles
Sandy Gap
Sinking River
Gravel Switch
Mammoth Cave
Barren River
Lakes

III Traffic Signs

Blue Signs — Regulate

Yellow Signs — Warn (Caution) — Mrs. S. E. Miller (Divided Highway
straight & NARE
TRAPS & SNARES
temptations)

Orange — School

Red Signs — Prohibit Movement
(stop, Don't Enter) (Yield   Stop — Ms. M. E. Hall (Body, mind, Soul
tellw when to
stop — ignore
sometimes)

Red/Black — No U Turn

Telephone (Blue & White) Ms. S. White telephone in
my bosom.

Orange (Construction

Green — Guide